Discovering Hitchin

Priscilla Douglas   Pauline Humphries

David Anopolos

A B Eastham   Derek Wheeler

Barry West

Stephen Bradford-RA   John Pearce

Pamela Saunders

Discovering Hitchin

An exploration of aspects of
Hitchin's history beyond
the town centre

Priscilla Douglas
and
Pauline Humphries

EGON

EGON PUBLISHERS LTD

Front endpapers: Aerial view of Hitchin, 1930s.

Half title: Photograph taken in March 1902 by Hitchin photographer H.G. Moulden at the Biggin Studio.

Frontispiece: Whinbush Road in the early years of the century.

Title page: 'The Hitchin Doctors' (1848) from a drawing by Samuel Lucas.

Page 7: Chapel of Caldicott School, Highbury Road.

Back endpapers: Aerial view of the Walsworth Road area, 1930s.

Copyright © Egon Publishers Ltd 1995

ISBN 0 905858 98 0

Designed by Nick Maddren
Campion Publishing Services, Baldock SG7 6DB
for Egon Publishers Ltd

Printed in England by
Streets Printers, Royston Road, Baldock, Herts SG7 6NW

Dedication

In memory of Ben Ward, a modern 'Hitchin Worthy'.

BEN WARD
1909 - 1993

Ben Ward was born in Hitchin on 21 August 1909 at 35 Florence Street. He attended St Saviour's and then The British Schools, leaving at fifteen to become a clerk for a local builder. In 1929 he began his long association with Willmotts where he rose through the ranks to end on the Board, retiring in 1972.

Ben was also a dedicated family man, and enthusiast for many town activities. He married Phyllis in 1941 and the family soon increased by two daughters, Rosemary and Angela, and an evacuee from Eastbourne, Herbert French.

Ben was active in support of the town's young people. He became closely involved with Hitchin Scouting and the Hitchin Youth Club. One of his proudest moments was to escort Her Majesty Queen Elizabeth the Queen Mother around the new Youth Centre in 1969.

Ben loved this town and developed a close interest in its history. He was involved with the Hitchin Society and the excavation of the Ice House in the Priory Park. Also, as a keen researcher, he became a member of the Hitchin Historical Society, inspired many of its members with his charm and enthusiasm and is still much missed at its meetings.

This volume is intended as an affectionate contribution to that tradition. We hope very much that Ben would have approved of it.

Contents

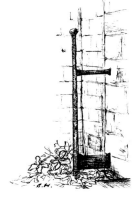

ACKNOWLEDGEMENTS

This book could not have been written without the help, so readily given, of the following:

Alison Taylor & Martin Roberts, of Hitchin Museum; Alan Fleck, Arts & Museums Officer, North Hertfordshire District Council; Steve Fletcher, local historian; The Librarians at Hitchin Public Library; The staff of the Hertfordshire Record Office; The staff of Leisure Services, North Hertfordshire District Council.

Specialist information has been provided by:

David Brooker, Maurice Burr, Mr B A J Chapman, Russ Craig, Matthew Day, Fiona Dodwell, William Heaton, Mr Cyril Jeffs, Doug King, John Ray and Mr & Mrs Theobald.

We would like to thank the residents of Hitchin, past and present, for their information, memories and photographs. Without their contributions this book could not have been written: Mrs Priscilla Arnold, Colin Brett, Mandy Brittany, Mrs Burnham, Mr & Mrs R B Cannon, Mrs Margaret Clarke, Mrs Nellie Coxall, Mr & Mrs B W G Ford, Mr Fyfe, John Godfrey, Mark Guest, Mrs Win Hare, Miss P J Hunt, Derek Larkins, Mrs K Linford, Mr & Mrs Maddox, Mrs H P Masters, Mrs Janet Masters-Boorman, Mr F W Matthews, Mr & Mrs N Mitchell, Mrs Pansy Mitchell, Mr John Murphy, Mr W J Palmer, Mr S. Pittman, Mrs Preston, Mrs Ivy Sainsbury, Mrs J Simmons, Mrs Edna Taylor, Mrs Ann Wheeler and Brian Worbey. Particular help was received from Jack Swain and the late Ron Perry.

We owe much to the discerning eyes of our illustrators: Mrs Daphne Gibson and Miss Becky Hull, also to Clarissa Szirtes and Mrs Jean Watts.

The work of our photographers, chiefly Peter Rollason and John Pearce, has added immeasurably to the value of the text. Special appreciation goes to the staff of the Photographic Department of Boots The Chemist (Hitchin) for their speed and efficiency in processing our many rolls of film.

Our gratitude is expressed to the members of Hitchin Historical Society for help in compiling the information contained in the book:

Dr Nigel Agar, Loretta Arnold, Mrs Mary Bradbeer, Mr Frank Chapman, Mrs Iris Clarke, Mr & Mrs Cole, Peter Currell, John Edwards, Ann Fitch, Chris Hubbard, Brian Limbrick, Mr Ben Nicholls, The Pearce Family, Don Studman, Robert Walmsley and Mrs Molly Wilson.

The following members have made extensive contributions to both research and text:

Stella Bousfield, Stephen Bradford-Best, David Chapallaz, Marshall Dellar, Derrick Else, Sue Fisher, Sue Fitzpatrick, David & Bridget Howlett, Laurie Hughes, Pam Maunders, Maya Pieris, The Skeggs Family, Kim Snell (junior member), Dr Gerry Tidy, Margaret Watson, and Barry West.

Especial thanks are due to Mrs Aud Eastham, Terry Knight and Derek Wheeler for their in-depth research and tenacity of purpose, and to our Chairman, David Howlett for his constructive suggestions. Our gratitude also to Sue Fitzpatrick and Bridget Howlett for their labour-intensive work on the Index.

We salute the sterling efforts of Dorothy Hughes, who, with unfailing patience and enthusiasm, transformed our often indecipherable prose into an ordered and readable form.

We are indebted to the patience of our partners and families who have borne the domestic imperfections of the past year with tolerance and good-humour.

Finally we would like to acknowledge the sympathetic encouragement of Nick Maddren, and of John Street, our publisher, whose interest and support have helped to make the writing of this book such a rewarding experience.

Priscilla Douglas
Pauline Humphries

FOREWORD

This book is not the product of any one author but of many. As such it is an appropriate tribute both to the Hitchin Historical Society, now in its eighteenth year, and to Ben Ward, one of its most dedicated and long standing members.

The Society is grateful to all those citizens of the town and the surrounding area who have responded so generously with their time, memories, photographs and other family treasures in order to make this latest contribution to the study of Hitchin's past possible.

The driving force behind the book - and the Chairman has chosen his words carefully here - has been Scilla Douglas and Pauline Humphries. It is an achievement in itself to gather the wide variety of material for a publication like this; it is an even greater achievement to weld it together into the fascinating and revealing account that it has become. I know they have both enjoyed the task immensely (even allowing for those of us who were late with our contributions!) but it

has still meant an enormous amount of hard work. Ben would have been proud of them.

Ben would also have been pleased that much of this book breaks new ground. We have deliberately chosen to look at areas and themes which have not received much attention in previous studies; little coverage is given here to the Town Centre and much more to a circuit of Hitchin's outer areas. You will see from the list of contents how, after some introductory topics, we start with Windmill Hill and then sweep through the suburbs and some related themes. In this way we aim to provide something complementary to the picture of the town's past that is usually presented.

Lastly, and this bears on both the fascination and the frustrations of undertaking research in local history, we wish to record that we have made every effort to verify the accuracy of the material we have included but, inevitably, some of you will know better.

Please remember that we did our best!

David Howlett, Fifth Chairman
October 1995

INTRODUCTION

The period covered by this book is, in historical terms, modern. Over the past 150 years Hitchin has enjoyed a period of unparalleled expansion and consolidation. As a thriving market town on the main road between London and Bedford, it had always been at the hub of local economic activity. With the arrival of the Great Northern Railway in 1850, and the Midland Railway soon afterwards, enormous impetus for change occurred. For the first time the town was provided with cheap and easy access to materials and markets.

Prosperity and opportunity drew workers to Hitchin. Workers needed houses, churches, schools and shops (not to mention public houses!). The compact medieval town surrounded by fields and market gardens was set to undergo profound change.

By 1901 the population had swelled to almost eleven thousand. The roads leading into the town were fringed with houses, and the area around the railway station had become a parish in it's own right, clustered round St. Saviour's Church. Housing development flourished at all economic and social levels. From the humble railway cottages by way of the respectable villas to the exclusive Gentleman's residence, change was everywhere.

Local builders employing local craftsmen brought their considerable skills to the task. Local materials were swelled by those brought in by rail. Ironfounders were kept hard at work, and the tradesmen of Hitchin, provided a constant supply of architectural furniture to adorn the new homes.

An appreciation of all this activity forms the core of our book. After a brief introduction to some topics of background interest, and to some useful facts and figures, we invite our readers to join us in a walk around suburban Hitchin. In the main we have tried to avoid those areas that have already been covered elsewhere. Although the route is circular we realise that some people might prefer to join the trail in their own neighbourhood, or to simply turn to an individual street.

We make no apology for the frequent diversions encountered along the way. Although many interesting things have vanished with the passage of time, the observant walker can still detect much about the former life of a street. We hope to have provided some clues.

We realise that some streets are covered in far more detail than others. Information has been gathered by many people, to the best of their ability, but much fascinating detail remains to be discovered. We hope that many of you will be encouraged to delve further into the histories of your own homes and streets. To this end we have added appendices after the main text.

Everybody who has contributed to this book has shared a common aim. We hope that all our readers will see the accustomed with new eyes and relish the real beauty and interest to be found on their own doorsteps.

Reproduced by kind permission of the Ordnance Survey, Southampton.
Crown copyright reserved 1925.

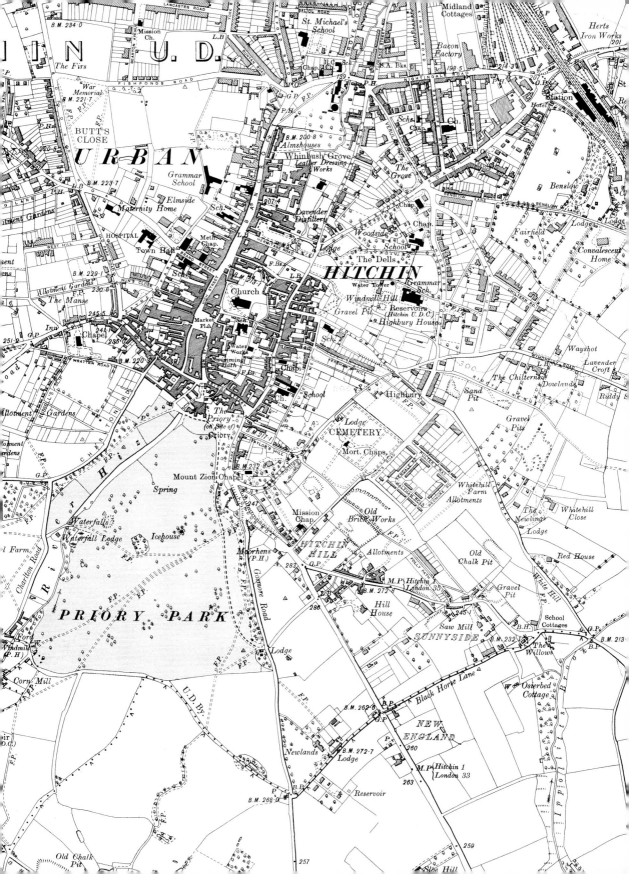

THE ORIGIN OF THE NAME

Hitchin is likely to have been named after the Hicce, an Anglo Saxon tribe that probably entered East Anglia along the rivers of the Wash and who settled in the area of northern Hertfordshire and southern Bedfordshire in the sixth century. The town became established as a central settlement for the tribe, although the extent of the territory probably owes as much to the lands attached to Ravensburgh hill fort in the Iron Age as to the Saxon invaders.

The precise origin of the name Hicce is, unfortunately, obscure and some academics have challenged its existence as a separate tribe; it appears as Hitche, Hicce and Hicche. The first written reference dates from the seventh century and its form subsequently varied over time. Hiz, now applied to one of our rivers, first appears in the Domesday Book of 1086 in the famous quotation 'Rex Wilhelm Tenet Hiz' (King William holds Hitchin). The modern name 'Hitchin' first appears in 1618 in a document called the Hertfordshire Feet of Fines. Even so, it has still been subject to variations since then. For example, Robert Morden's map of Hertfordshire of about 1690 describes the town as 'Hitching'; by the time Thomas Moule prepared his county maps in the 1830's the modern form was firmly established although even today sharp-eyed residents may spot 'Hitchen' in occasional use.

> **What's in a name?**
> Through the centuries Hitchin has had various names . . .
> Hicca, Hiz, Hychene, Hychh, Hycke, Hyche, Hucche, Hechen, Hicche, Hacche, Hycchyn, Hich, Hiche, Hechyn, Huchyn, Huthe, Huchine, Hytchen, Hitching, Hitche.
> There are various theories on how the town gained its name but none is conclusive.

Left: The Lion symbolises the royal manor of Hitchin. The sheaf of barley, the sheep and crooks and the tanner's fleshing knife represent important elements of the economy of the town and its markets.

Above: 'Both for our ancestors and our posterity.'
Right: A sketch by Samuel Lucas from Hine's
Hitchin Countryside*: 'Jogging Home from The Farmer's Audit'.*

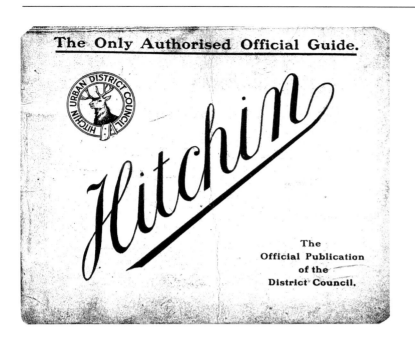

The Only Authorised Official Guide.

Hitchin

The Official Publication of the District Council.

Left: Guide of 1910.
Below: Souvenir spoon from the 1980's.

ANCIENT SEAL OF HERTFORD

HITCHIN.

REGD TRADE MARK.
HERALDIC SERIES.

Above: Blue trinket box with gold lettering and quilted red interior made at the turn of the century, and bought to contain a small gift.

REMINDERS OF THE URBAN DISTRICT COUNCIL

In a nation like ours, with a tradition of centuries of settled administration, local government has long been an important contributor to local identity. Inhabitants usually consider themselves as 'coming from' a particular place and that location is frequently the focus for their work, basic economic needs, the education of their children and their social activities. In England ancient ecclesiastical parishes normally came to provide the basic unit of local administration, although parishes themselves often had roots in remote antiquity as shown by the evidence for many of their old established boundaries. Towns and villages, which were the natural centres of local parishes, also became the homes of local administration. Hitchin was one such centre with an independent administrative identity based on the overlapping of manorial and parish regulation stretching back to before 1066 and only ended by the local government changes of 1974.

By the eighteenth century, when the country was on the verge of the economic and social transformation that forged modern Britain, the great majority of the inhabitants would have identified the parish as the most important unit of administration that affected their daily lives. By then the parish had come to be governed by a 'vestry' committee, presumably named after the area of the church in which it originally met. It was usually a self-perpetuating group composed of the most prosperous local citizens under the chairmanship of the parson. The importance of the vestry had become wider than religious affairs and its decisions ranged from allocating the pews in the parish church to making detailed welfare provision for poor and elderly widows, apprenticing pauper children and keeping an eye on the state of the local roads and on the overseers of the poor in conjunction with the county justices. As agricultural changes gathered pace and steadily eroded the manor's organising functions in local affairs, the Vestries took on responsibility for more and more. They were also supplemented, in an ad hoc way, by new agencies such as Turnpike Trusts and Poor Law Guardians.

Hitchin was no exception to these trends. Under the Public Health Act of 1848 the town formally became an administrative parish and a Local Board was established on 19 March 1850. Unfortunately the Board did not proceed smoothly, becoming embroiled in political and financial rows through the introduction of an unsatisfactory water and sewerage system for the town. Board members refused to take responsibility for the debt, so between 1859 and 1873 the town was governed by committees of ratepayers (readers are referred to Tony Foster's *Market Town* for an account of these difficulties). The Board was refounded in 1873 and formed the basis for the Hitchin Urban District Council established under the Local Government Act of 1894 which created a more systematic and democratic form of local administration.

The first HUDC elections took place on 19 December 1894 and, as a reflection that some things in our national life change little, the Hertfordshire Express complained 'There was so little interest taken.... that only about one fourth of the electors took the trouble to record their votes'. The new Council, which began work the following year, comprised twelve members of which four retired annually. It met fortnightly on Wednesdays at 6.00pm in the Council Room at the (old) Town Hall. There was much continuity between the Board and the UDC and the 1894 elections returned many men whose surnames are still familiar in the town – Jeeves, Halsey, Ransom and Hill. W O Times became Clerk to the Council; on

Just "a line" from **Hitchin**.

Above: Postcard stamped 1917.
Right: Postcard dated 6th August 1922: St Mary's Church and war memorial.

retirement in 1925 he had completed fifty-two years service to the Local Board and then the UDC. The UDC was soon marked by the commissioning of the New Town Hall, opened on 18 March 1901 by Mrs Hudson, wife of the MP for Hitchin. The cost of the scheme was about £7,300 and the civic spirit of several of the town's leading inhabitants was marked by the gift of the land by William and Alfred Ransom, Frederic Seebohm, W O Times and the trustees of J. H. Tuke. Civic pride went hand in hand with a strong sense of continuity; when the Hermitage Road box trees were felled Mr Barker presented the UDC with a gavel and block made from some of their wood.

The creation of the UDC reflected national trends encouraging increased intervention by local government in local affairs. Initially the UDC took on the responsibilities of the Local Board in relation to the fabric of the town and attempted to further its involvement. For example the Council attempted to buy the Hitchin Gas Company in 1905 (it helped that W O Times was at one time a director of the company), in 1902 it obtained powers to supply electricity within the town, a new cattle market was established in 1903, the Windmill Hill water tower and reservoir inaugurated in

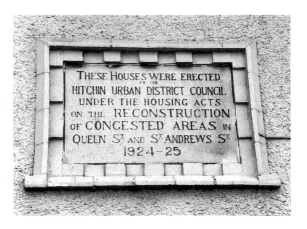

Below: Hydrant cover to be seen in Bearton Road.

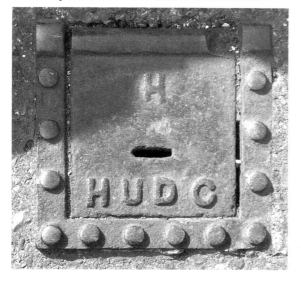

Top: Plaque can be seen on the Sunnyside Estate.
Below: Crest above pool in Fishponds Road.

1909 and in 1910 improvements were made to the sewage works.

Hitchin's local worthies seem generally to have been satisfied with the standard of government they provided for the town. In December 1894 Mr Stevens, who headed the poll for the new UDC Councillors, noted with satisfaction that '... if at the end of the next twenty-one years, so much could be said in favour of the Urban District Council as has now been said in favour of the Local Board nobody will be able to throw stones at it...'. Not everyone agreed, however, and the Hertfordshire Express soon contained a complaint about the delays in making up

Victoria Road off Lucas Lane '... and some other features in ...the Council's ...unfortunate career...' penned by 'Agitator' and rounded off with an amusing acrostic:

V is the Vow which the Council did make,
I is the Intention it formed but to break
C is our Chagrin that such course it should take,
T is our Theory, the Council's gone wrong,
O is the Ousting it'll get before long,
R is the Rejoicing when true comes this song,
I are the Improvements proposed but not made,
A plans Amended but still in the shade.

R anxious Ratepayers of high rates afraid,
O the Objection to too fine a hall,
A the Alarm lest it be mean and small,
D the grave Doubts if we get one at all!

Expectations rose and local councils had to provide an increasing array of services.

HITCHIN

H
E
R
T
F
O
R
D
S
H
I
R
E

" ...a township like this of Hitchin, 'not wholly in the busy world nor quite beyond it' , ...

Tucked away in the northern-most corner of Hertfordshire, we maintain our calm and settled security, our home-bred virtues, our local attachments. We are tempted occasionally to make a stir in the world, but prefer on the whole to abide as a modest country town, lying out of the highway of innovation and having the quaint seal of antiquity upon its title deeds. For centuries we have preserved this serenity of character, which has always attracted the strangers to our Gates."

REGINALD HINE

Road sign recording the links forged with Germany in the late 1950s and with France in the early 1970s.

National legislation of 1909 initiated the first steps in town planning but it was after 1920 that the UDC was most active. Amidst national calls of 'Homes fit for Heroes' it tackled the slum housing of Queen Street, allegedly some of the worst in the county. The area was cleared (an event still marked by an inscription on the St Mary's Square steps) and new public housing was developed at Sunnyside, off Woolgrove Road and Mattocke Road during the 1920's; by 1967 the UDC had provided about 2,400 new dwellings. The UDC hoped to develop a new shopping area around St Mary's Square but the scheme remained firmly on the drawing board.

The Council was active in many other areas from providing a new open air swimming pool (1937-38), establishing the Library (1938) and, with the Hitchin Regional Survey, the Museum (1941), to the making of footpaths in the town and the regular production of a Hitchin District Guide for visitors. Towards the end of its life it was also a pioneer of conservation areas and architectural awards in a scheme devised for the historic town centre. Although it is over twenty years since the UDC ceased to exist many traces of its activity remain.

Crested China

Most towns and cities are situated on historical sites and throughout the nineteenth century several of these were excavated during rebuilding works. A surprising number of pottery and porcelain items were discovered, most of which ended up in their local museums. The Falcon Pottery, founded by William Henry Goss in the 1850's at Stoke-on-Trent, was the first to capitalise on these ancient relics when in the 1880's the founder's son, Adolphous Goss became a director. His hobby was heraldry and he persuaded his father to introduce a new range of fine china items bearing coats of arms. Thus those familiar little bits of nonsense, that everyone's aunt and grandmother once displayed so proudly in their china cabinets, were conceived.

Above: A model of the posset cup displays a hart on a blue background.
Right: Advertisement from the Hitchin Directory of 1915.

Originally only objects relating to a particular area and bearing the relevant crest or coat of arms were produced. In the case of Hitchin there is only one local piece that the Goss factory made and that is the Posset Cup, the original of which was found in the town. (A posset is a drink of hot milk with wine, spices etc., once popular as a remedy for colds).

These little trifles proved enormously popular with the general public for they were ideal gifts or mementos from a favourite holiday place and people soon began to collect a piece from each place they visited. So popular were they that the factory increased its output to meet the demand and from this time crests from towns, boroughs, Royalty and the aristocracy were used on all items irrespective of their eventual retailing destination. The most valuable Goss items bear a matching crest but other items were produced, perhaps most famously their cottages which because of their comparatively small rate of production and their price, were not bought in the same numbers as their little pots.

Above: This local collection includes some interesting items from the First World War. Right: Early postcard depicts the interest in crested china.

Goss china is easily distinguished by the markings on the underside of the models and one should look for the wording 'W H Goss", or the illustration of their trade mark a Gosshawk. The Company continued to produce their crested ware for many years and the collecting craze was at its height up until the 1920's but the quality of the porcelain - which was of the finest at one time - became rather poor towards the end of the factory's life in 1944.

Other companies were quick to follow the success of the Goss factory but as a general rule the quality was inferior. Some of the manufacturers were: Arcadian, Grafton, Carlton, Willow and Shelley. Interestingly, Goss china was also illustrated on a set of postcards issued by S Oates & Company in the early 1900's.

HITCHIN POST

The sending of letters or messages was formalised by King Henry VIII and was officially opened to the public by King Charles I in 1635 with the founding of the Royal Mail. The General Post Office (GPO), responsible for the sorting of all letters to provincial towns, was established by Oliver Cromwell in 1657. Around this time letter-receiving houses were opened in smaller towns, usually in shops and eating places.

The first reference to Hitchin in the establishment book of the GPO was in 1756, but the first Hitchin postmaster to be recorded was William Marshall in 1760. He was the proprietor of the Sun Hotel in Sun Street, probably Hitchin's first post office. His

Unusual early postcard containing a pull-out strip of local views.

SOMETHING FOR YOU FROM HITCHIN

Within this postman's bag you'll find An interesting gift consigned.

Regd. No. 569368   834

successor was Richard Barry, also the proprietor of the Sun Hotel. The postmasters of this era were usually appointed under the patronage of the local Member of Parliament. The first mail coaches were introduced in 1784 between London and Bristol. In 1786 a service was introduced between London and York and letters were relayed to and from Baldock by local post boys. In 1791 Isaac Coxall became postmaster, probably from premises in Cock Street (now High Street). He developed a more organised system of local delivery. He was followed in 1800 by William Dunnage, a grocer and tallow chandler, also in Cock Street. He was also an amateur local historian. The first postmistress in Hitchin was Mrs Ball, who was appointed in 1832. By this date Hitchin had finally become a post town and received daily deliveries of letters by the Royal Mail. Coach services to the north from London actually travelled through Hitchin. In 1837 John Palmer, a bookseller and stationer, again in Cock Street, was appointed postmaster. A copy invoice including that his business was also the post office can be seen. There had been several increases in the postal rates over the years which were based more on raising revenue for the government than being related to the postal service. In 1791 the cost of a letter sent to London had risen to four pence and by 1814 to seven pence. The next major change to postal services came in 1839 with the introduction of the 'Uniform Penny Post' following a report to government by Rowland Hill. A penny post system had been set up in London as early as 1680 and this arrangement had also been used in other cities and large provincial towns. Now the system was adopted nationally. In the following year postage stamps - the 'penny black' - and prepaid envelopes with a picture of Britannia were first used. Postage was now within everyone's reach. Sixty-eight million 'penny black' stamps were sold in the first ten months of their issue.

In addition to the main post office in Cock Street a sub post office was opened by Michael Chapman in Portmill Lane to sell stamps. A further sub post office was opened at a later date in Station Road (now Walsworth Road). The issue of stamps and prepaid envelopes combined with the provision of a letter box in the door of the post office allowed you to send letters even when the post office was closed.

In 1853 the post office moved to the premises of Samuel Tomson, a printer and binder in Bucklersbury and, following the sudden death of his successor George Bentley only seven months after his appointment, moved yet again this time to Number Two Market Place on the appointment of John Beaver. The post office remained at his grocery store for forty years and was extended in 1890. During his term as postmaster the number of letters delivered in Hitchin increased dramatically. In 1859 there were five thousand but by 1897 the number had increased to twenty-one thousand. The railways were a major factor in the expansion and efficiency of the postal service. Mr Beaver employed several postmen including Henry Worsley in the town and Mr Whitehead and Mr Hobbs to cover the rural areas. Mr Aylott and Mr

The Sale family lived at Hinxworth Place for many generations.

Upchurch were also employed during this period. Mr Upchurch commenced his duty at 6.30am and walked via Preston and Kings Walden to Bendish. He would blow a whistle at designated places to call for outgoing mail. He would not return to his home until after 7.30pm. Mr Whitehead covered the Walsworth, Willian and Letchworth areas. He would blow a horn rather than a whistle although in his later years, when he had run out of puff, he would ring a bell. The Sailor Boy public house in Walsworth was the last place he called for outgoing mail. The increase in the number of letters to be delivered, and the expansion of the town, caused the local authority to ensure

The new post office and the Wesleyan Chapel in Brand Street (postcard 1905).

Above left: Type 'B' box intended for Nigeria. Centre: 'Airmail' box in Old Hale Way. Right: Type 'C' box in Hermitage Road.

that all the houses in each street and road were numbered to aid identification. Previously vague descriptions were often used like 'the house with the yellow door opposite the pond'. It also encouraged householders to provide a letter box in their front door. In 1860 the first post boxes appeared in Hitchin. The first post boxes had been erected in London in 1853. The first ones in Hitchin were in Old Park Road, Nightingale Road and 'Hitchin Hill' and later in Bancroft, Tilehouse Street, The Avenue, Hermitage Road and at the railway station. The standard pillar boxes painted red were introduced in 1876 but none remain in Hitchin. The only Victorian post box which remains is mounted in the wall of a former shop in Old Park Road.

By 1889 there were four deliveries in the town each day. An example of a Hitchin postmark can be seen on the envelope addressed to Mrs Sale of Hinxworth. Uniforms had been introduced around 1793 including a 'beaver', a top hat with a turned up brim. A flat round hat was introduced in 1859 and was replaced by a military-style peaked cap in 1862. Trousers were first issued to all provincial postmen at this time. In 1898 a double peaked 'shako' type helmet was introduced with a blue shiny front and cloth rear. The first full-time postmaster was appointed in 1900, Mr J Willis. He was the postmaster when the post office moved to new premises in Brand Street, purpose built by M Foster & Co. in 1904 . The first motor van was used by the GPO in Hitchin in the same year.

Succeeding postmasters included Mr F J Batho in 1907 and Howard Tomkyns in 1922. When he arrived one hundred and fifty nine staff were employed at Hitchin Post Office and three motor cycle combinations were in use, but by the time he retired in 1934 there were three hundred and twenty four staff, five motor cycle combinations and nine motor vans. The number of letters delivered had risen to more than fifty two thousand. Details of the latest posting times in Hitchin can be found in an extract from the Hitchin Household Almanack and Directory in 1926 . In 1927 the sorting office was opened in Kings Road and in 1932 the postman's hat was changed again, this time to a flat rounded peak cap. At his retirement presentation ceremony, Mr Howlett, the Stevenage postmaster, said of Mr Tomkyns that '..... he knew how to find fault (with his sub officers) in a courteous, gentle and helpful manner'. He was replaced by Robert Wigglesworth.

The first sixpenny telegram service was introduced in 1935 and the first telegram was taken for despatch by the local messenger, Kenneth Howard, for Mrs Wiggs, wife of the Chairman of the Council. The number of daily deliveries had reduced to three by this time and shortly after the Second World War a further reduction to two deliveries was introduced. In 1948 the average number of letters delivered had increased to one hundred and seventeen thousand. Many more post and pillar boxes were introduced in existing areas and also on new estates as the town expanded further into the countryside. A list of 'pillar boxes' can be found in the 1952/53 Hitchin Directory. Most of them are the standard type 'B' box but some, including the ones in Market Place, Bedford Road and Bancroft, are the larger type 'A' box. The Bancroft post box used to be set in a brick pillar close to the kerb and was regularly clipped by Dr Marshall Gilbertson as he reversed his pretty Singer coupé from his home at number 30 into the street. We have a few unusual post boxes in Hitchin, two not immediately apparent. The type 'B' box in Conquest Close was intended for Nigeria but somehow found its way to Hitchin. It differs from similar boxes by having a plain, rather than a fluted, rim to the top of the box. There is a similar one in Ickleford. The pillar box in Old Hale Way started off life as an 'Air Mail' box on another site and was painted blue. Where it was originally sited is not known. There are several similar pedestal boxes around the town like the one in Pirton Road although the pedestals often differ in shape - large and small tubular post and angular metal. There are no Edward VIII post boxes in Hitchin, although many exist around the country, but there are two examples of Edward VII boxes, a type 'B' in Wymondley Road and the type 'A' in Market Place. There are several George V boxes, including those in Bunyan Road and London Road and also several George VI post boxes including those in Periwinkle Lane and The Avenue. The majority of the postboxes, both pillar and pedestal, are Elizabeth II although there are only three of the modern type 'K' pillar boxes, originally introduced in 1980, in Blackhorse Lane, Coleridge Close and Hollow Lane. An unusual type 'C' oval pillar box now stands outside the redundant main post office in Hermitage Road. It has two apertures originally intended for first and second class post but the labels have been covered over to allow double capacity for either class of post. The post and sorting office moved to the premises in Hermitage Road in 1962 and was considered to be a model site. The then postmaster Charles Morris can remember with pride showing visitors from Britain and abroad around the modern buildings which included a vehicle maintenance depot. The move towards privatisation of the Post Office resulted in the Counter Services, now known as Post Office Counters Limited, being separated from the postal services, known as Royal Mail. New post boxes now have ROYAL MAIL cast on them instead of POST OFFICE. There is no longer a post office owned by the Post Office in Hitchin although the sorting office was still in use to sort local mail in 1995.

Early miniature post box bought at Boots Chemists. It contained an aromatic strip for the sickroom.

Postcards

Readers will have noticed that this book is generously illustrated by old postcards and it is thanks to the photographers and shopkeepers in the early years of this century that such a wealth of material is available. Of course the collectors of postcards played perhaps the most important part by preserving the invaluable pictorial information depicted on these fascinating scraps of paper.

The exact date of the issue of the first picture postcard is still a subject for debate but 1869 is generally accepted as the year and Austria the country which pioneered the service. The first British card followed a year later but this was a plain card with a printed stamp which gave the card a distinctly official look.

It was not until 1st September 1894 that picture postcards were allowed to be used in this country and these first cards were small, measuring 4.5" x 3.5" and were known as Court Cards. In 1902 the Post Office allowed the backs of postcards to be divided, thus allowing both the address and the message to appear on the same side. This in turn enabled the front of the card to be devoted solely to the picture and it was from this date that the craze of collecting picture postcards began. Britain was the first country to adopt the divided back and the rest of the world soon followed. At this time the standardisation of card size was introduced at 5.5" x 3.5".

Local photographers worked tirelessly to record every worthwhile and trivial event that happened in their locality. Processions, sieges, pageants, disasters, civic and royal visits, fairs etc were all faithfully photographed. Local views featuring animated street scenes with buildings now long demolished and local services such as firemen, police and railway workers are particularly interesting to historians. The collecting craze continued until the outbreak of the First World War with huge numbers of cards passing through the postal service, for example in 1908 over 860 million cards were delivered. In the early years of the century

BINDING WORKS, PARCELL'S YARD, BUCKLERSBURY.

Paternoster and Hales,

Bookbinders and Account Book Manufacturers,

MARKET PLACE AND SUN STREET, HITCHIN.

Table and Desk Tops Covered and Ornamented.   Maps, Plans, &c.
Mounted and Varnished.   Prices and specimens on application.

Advertisement from the Handbook to Hitchin of 1899.

there were several deliveries a day in populated areas and such was the reliability of the service that a card could be posted in the morning advising the addressee that the sender would be arriving on such and such a train later that day with the certain confidence that it would be delivered on time.

The 'Golden Age', as it is known in the collecting fraternity, finally came to an end with the doubling of the postal rate in 1918. This, coupled with the spread of the private telephone and greater mobility with the expansion of motor traffic, led to a lessening

Right: Waterside abuts Bridge Street early in the century. Note the delivery boy from Garratts Fishmongers in Brand Street.

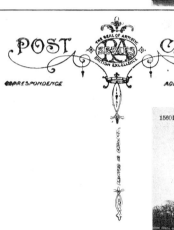

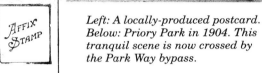

Left: A locally-produced postcard. Below: Priory Park in 1904. This tranquil scene is now crossed by the Park Way bypass.

demand and also a decline in general standards of production.

Although millions of albums were discarded to the dustbin when their original owners died, enough survive to nurture the growing body of keen collectors – many of them young people who have discovered the fascination of ephemera.

Among the many local retailers who commissioned postcards from the town's photographers were:

R H Kingston of Station Road, Jeweller, Stationer & Bookseller

A E Lupton, 141 Nightingale Road
W Smith, Brand Street and High Street
Carling & Hales Ltd., 27 Market Place (later Paternoster & Hales)
Latchmore, Photographer
Mack Studios, 18 Bearton Road
H G Moulden, Hitchin
C Waldock, Market Place
H Odell, Printer & Stationer, Nightingale Road, Hitchin
T. Issott, Hitchin
Herbert H. Minnis, Hitchin

ALLEYS AND FOOTPATHS

One of the features of Hitchin that makes the town such an interesting place is its network of alleys and footpaths which extend over the whole area. An exploration of these gives a new view of the town, its buildings, development and the people who have shaped its history.

An explanation of why there are so many of these by-ways is given by Aillie Latchmore in her book *People, Places and Past Times of Hitchin,* published in 1974. She recalls William Ransom, the founder of Wm. Ransom & Son, the pharmaceutical chemists in Bancroft, telling her that he owned a great deal of land and property in the town, as did Miss Wilshere, a devout churchwoman. She objected to Mr Ransom's views as a Quaker and she had space left wherever their properties met and had a fence put up or a large hedge planted on her side. These spaces were soon used as short cuts by the townspeople and became rights of way.

Rural boundaries always used to be marked by a ditch and a hedge - the ditch outside the hedge so there might be some truth in the Ransom/Wilshere tale. Although some alleys and footpaths do form boundaries between different properties, they also exist for a number of other reasons. Several are old through-routes, roads and lanes, now no longer part of the road network. Others are more recent, laid out by the developers to link the new suburbs with the town or station. For some people a footpath is or was the only access to their property. Some of the paths combine several of these features.

The alleys and footpaths in five areas of the town are grouped together to illustrate their many different origins and we will deal with each of these areas in turn. It should be noted, however, that not every alley and footpath is mentioned although the great majority are covered to a greater or lesser extent.

An old HUDC signpost in Wilbury Way.

The Town Centre or The Medieval Core

The first footpath we will consider is Taylor's Hill, which runs from Park Street to Standhill Road. On the 1898 Ordnance Survey map of Hitchin, Standhill Road is still known as Cemetery Road. Taylor's Hill is one of the footpaths in the town where houses front it and that is their only access.

Storehouse Lane is an unmade footpath and goes from Taylor's Hill to St Andrew's Place. It appears to be a form of back lane to Queen Street and as such can be thought of being an outer boundary of Hitchin's medieval core.

Lyle's Row is a very short footpath, which runs from St Andrew's Place to Queen Street, passing the side of the laundry which ceased business earlier this year.

The next footpath we shall look at is another short one. It goes from Hermitage Road to Portmill Lane. The River Hiz runs parallel to it and the town's former Port Mill stood where the water drops in order to flow under the road. It is interesting to note that the back garden of Frederic Seebohm's house, the Hermitage, occupied the area before the

Two views, fifty years apart:
Above: Lyle's Row, which leads
off Queen Street.
Left: A photograph taken by
Arthur Codling in about 1960,
showing the view from
Kershaw's Hill looking
towards Queen Street.

construction of Hermitage Road in 1874.

Moving on, we come to Churchyard, which runs from Market Place to Moss's Corner. We shall actually call it Churchyard West for want of a better name. It follows the line of the huge original market area which, at one time, occupied that part of the town now bounded by Bancroft, High Street, Bucklersbury and Sun Street through to Tilehouse Street, in addition, of course, to Market Place itself, until recently used as a car park prior to its re-development as a pedestrianised area.

The next footpath, Churchyard Walk, the north side of the churchyard, goes from Churchyard and through what was the former Church House garden to St Mary's Square and is still on church land.

Yet another footpath in the immediate area is also known as Churchyard Walk, but which

we shall call Churchyard South. It has modern shops running along one side of it and these face the south part of the church. The whole churchyard area, with shops opening onto it, is a classic form which is not often seen nowadays.

We will now look at Munt's Alley, which runs from Oliver's shoe shop in the High Street to Howell's newsagents which closed earlier this year. The alley takes it name from Munt's pram and toy shop which preceded Oliver's. It has two dog legs along its length and is almost certainly a property boundary within the market infill. Its walls have been re-decorated recently, giving it a much improved appearance and smell!

In contrast is the very short narrow alley which runs in a straight line further up High Street to Churchyard nearer to Moss's Corner.

This photograph of West Alley, taken in the early 1960s, shows some of the buildings which stood on the site of the one-time flourishing antiques market.

A Passage from High Street to the Churchyard, 1899.

Above: Etching by Frederick L. Griggs, born in Hitchin in 1876. Left: Churchyard, looking towards the area once known as Golden Square, early in the century.

This was once known as Aram's Alley after Eugene Aram, an usher at the nearby Church School in the eighteenth century. He was hanged for murder and his ghost was said to haunt this passageway.

West Alley, formerly Cod-piece Alley, then Quaker's Alley, goes from the High Street to Paynes Park. It probably had its origin as a footpath along the edge of a burgage plot, the narrow property fronting the High Street. Hitchin's Quakers had their Meeting Place here - on the site of the antiques market - until a new one was erected in Bedford Road which, in turn, was succeeded by the modern building at the junction of Bedford Road and Paynes Park.

Only a few yards distant from where West Alley and Paynes Park meet is another path-cum-alley which goes from Paynes Park, behind Brooker's Yard, past the former Guild Rooms and out into Tilehouse Street. It, too, has a couple of dog legs along its length and

was probably a property boundary (in the same way as Munt's Alley). It was formerly known as Queen's Head Passage after a former public house in Tilehouse Street, although it is not absolutely certain on which corner of the path it stood.

The last footpath in this group is now a very short one, running from Queen's Head Passage to the Hine Memorial Garden, formerly the site of the Free School. Part of this path was cut across when the by-pass was built.

The West Side or Where Town meets Country.

This area illustrates the edge of the town where traditionally-used agricultural land has been taken over for urban development.

The first footpath to be considered is Braund's Alley, which runs from Old Park Road, opposite the Library, to Gray's Lane. It does not appear on the 1844 Tithe Map for

Footpath between Bearton Green and Bedford Road showing a length of its interesting wall.

Hitchin but it is on the 1898 Ordnance Survey map. It is thought to have taken its name from Albert Braund, who had a wine and spirit business in Old Park Road. On one side of the path was the Manse belonging to Tilehouse Street Baptist Church and part of the garden wall still exists.

Russell's Slip starts at Wratten Road and continues to the open space as one approaches Hawthorne Close. The houses that exist along its length were doubtless erected on a single strip of land in the old open fields, but it is strange how this small development came about, as the area would have been very remote from the rest of the town. Incidently, a 'slip' simply means a long narrow piece of ground, but which Russell it was remains a mystery!

At this point it might not be inappropriate to mention the long narrow unsurfaced path which runs from Moormead Hill to Pirton Road, behind the wall that belonged to Rosenberg House, now replaced by Tudor Court.

The next footpath to consider is Lucas Lane, which is the longest in Hitchin. Strictly speaking, it begins at Pirton Road where the first stretch is known as Crow Furlong. It then continues along the top of Gray's Lane, West Hill, Gaping Lane, Lavender Way and Victoria Road before crossing Oughtonhead Way to go on past the top of Maxwell's Path, Fosman Close and Berkeley Close before it ends at Redhill Road. Lucas Lane can be considered to be a natural rather than an actual boundary of the town. It is on a ridge and provided access to fields.

Chalkdell Path runs from Oughtonhead Way to Maxwell's Path. It appears on the 1844 Tithe Map as one block of land. The houses that run along its length were built on part of it, with their gardens in front and the path itself is their only approach.

Maxwell's Path begins at Lucas Lane and runs to Bedford Road. Part of it is a genuine right of way and a section now has vehicular access. However, by looking closely at the tarmac, it can be seen that this stretch was also a footpath.

The North Side: Old Rights of Way and New Developments

This part of Hitchin starts near the town centre and goes out as far as Old Hale Way. Only one path, Elmside Walk, has a name; the remainder need to be defined from where they start to where they finish. Elmside Walk runs from Bedford Road to Butts Close and then to Fishponds Road. It is parallel to Grammar School Walk and has taken the function of this road which, as a footpath, would have continued across what is the Boys' School land, now inaccessible to the public.

Moving on, the path from Fishponds Road to York Road, emerges by Foskett's butcher's shop. This may well have originated as part of the back lane along the edge of the town, going to Ickleford, but then became adopted as the back route to the houses in Bunyan Road when they were built.

The path from York Road to Bearton Avenue is parallel to Lancaster Road and runs behind Wilshere Dacre School. It does not appear on the 1898 Ordnance Survey map so it can be assumed that it was laid out when the houses were erected in order that they could be serviced from the rear.

At the junction of Lancaster Avenue and Lancaster Road is a path which leads to Bearton Road and this is the boundary between the fields on which these streets were developed.

The public right of way from Brampton Park Road to Strathmore Avenue is doubtless another remnant of an old route which was kept when the area was being built up.

Last but not least is the path that runs from Bearton Green to Bedford Road. It is very short, but it has what at least two local historians describe as an 'absolutely wonderful' wall running along one side of it. This wall was clearly put up at the same time as the houses in Bearton Green, between the wars, when there was a shortage of bricks and so any kind of material that was to hand was used, including clinker from local iron foundries.

The North-East Side or Nineteenth Century Suburban Development

The first path in this group is Burton's Path which runs from Station Approach to Benslow Lane. It then becomes Avenue Path, which runs from the opposite side of Benslow Lane, crossing The Avenue and finishing at Highbury Road.

Another path runs from Benslow Lane, at the back of Pinehill Hospital to the edge of Chiltern Road, now called Pinehill Path (invented or rediscovered?)

A third path runs from further along Chiltern Road, across The Avenue and Highbury Road and then alongside the Girls' School and The Dell by Windmill Hill to Queen Street.

These paths originated during the development of the area at the turn of the century to enable the middle-class commuters easy access to the station. There is a parallel between this development and that in Benslow Rise which, although much later, has its own footpath to the station.

The South-East Side or Agriculture & Industry

The first path in this group runs from St Andrew's Place to St John's Road as Kershaw's Hill and Kershaw's Path. It appears on the 1898 Ordnance Survey map running between two rows of allotments.

Riddy Path is next. It runs from Hollow Lane and then at the back of Wymondley Road to Manor Crescent on the Oakfield Estate. This is a genuine right of way, being clearly marked on modern maps. Although it is now a back lane, it was probably once a major route out of the town to the fields.

Another path runs from Whitehill Road to Stevenage Road and is probably similar in origin to Folly Path which runs from Stevenage Road to St John's Road. This goes through the old brickworks, which appear on the 1898 Ordnance Survey map, and is on a causeway so it appears to be a pre-existing right-of-way that had to be maintained. The brickworks were on the site of the present day playing fields.

Go up and down Hitchin Hill Path and Butchers Lane which run between London Road and Stevenage Road. The houses here date from the eighteenth century and would have formed a separate little hamlet at that time.

The last footpath we will look at is St John's Path, which goes from St John's Road to Standhill Road. It has houses facing onto it in a similar way to those already noted in Chalkdell Path and in Taylor's Hill.

Avenue Path: The initials 'G.W.R.' stand for G.W. Russell, the owner of the land. Local legend reports a dispute between him and the adjacent landowner.

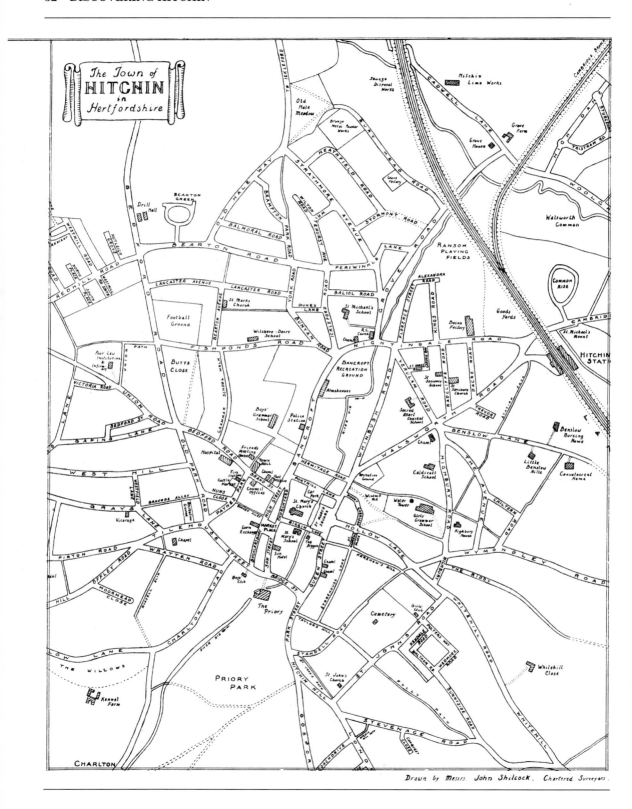

Drawn by Messrs. John Shilcock, Chartered Surveyors.

Down the streets where we live . . .

Listen awhile to these dear, friendly garrulous, gossipy old houses that will talk and talk and talk if only you will let them; listen with your heart as well as your ears, and you will discover that not only are they comely and well-wrought, but informed with a living spirit, and packed full of memories.

Reginald L Hine

HIGHBURY RD HITCHIN.

WINDMILL HILL

As the name implies this is the site of one of Hitchin's former landmarks, the mill belonging to James Hack Tuke. It caught fire on 7 November 1875 and the combined efforts of the Hitchin Fire Brigade with their manual fire engine and the townspeople failed to quench the flames. The friction generated when windmills are subjected to gales has been the cause of many a mill's downfall. The miller's cottage stood on the Hollow Lane side of the hill until the early 1950's.

In the early part of the last century the hill was known as Rawlings Hill, after a former owner of the mill. Later in the century, the land was bought by Frederic Seebohm, the Quaker banker, who lived down the hill in the Hermitage, facing on to Bancroft. Dug into the top of the hill is the water reservoir, first coming into use on the 3 May 1853, and feeding the town by gravity. The water was pumped from the old Waterworks building in Queen Street by a steam engine. The water tower, which is still visible, but now topless, was built in 1909. Seebohm, who was a great benefactor to the town, owned an estate which included the present Hermitage Road, and the whole of Windmill Hill as far as Hollow Lane. He sacrificed part of his garden to make the 'New Road' as it was called in 1875, now known as Hermitage Road, and later, in 1907, gave land at the top for the building of Hitchin Girls' Grammar School. His two daughters, Esther and Hilda, gave the rest of the hill to the town in 1921. It must be remembered that a prominent local businessman, John Barker, had a house built on the hill in the early 1920's and apparently made himself very unpopular at the time, having the best view in Hitchin. Incidently the first electric cooker in Hitchin was fitted in his house, powered by the old electricity works in Whinbush Road.

In winter the hill becomes a focus for sledging and occasionally skis appear. Wooden sledges have largely given way to plastic creations but for those to whom snow comes as a surprise, estate agents' boards, milk crates, bread trays, black plastic bags and even a seven seater tarpaulin prove to be ready substitutes.

There used to be iron railings at the foot of the hill, but it is recounted that a young lad was impaled on them after a particularly rapid descent. Chains with spikes were a later hazard, but waste bins and seats seem to provide adequate emergency braking systems nowadays. The odd casualty still occurs, but the pedestrian fencing must surely prevent a continuous 'Cresta Run' down Hermitage Road. At the same time of the year, local lads seem to take a pride in seeing if they can snowball their mates across the traffic from the foot of the hill to the frontage of the dry cleaners. Unfortunately this year a snowball went through the open window of a police car and the winter sports enthusiasts witnessed the constabulary give spirited chase between slithering cars in Hermitage Road!

The hill is a popular area in the summer when townsfolk and school pupils meet in their lunch hours. How many Hitchin partnerships first met on this pleasant spot?

In this age of sexual equality one must make a comment about the provision of public conveniences in Hitchin. Did our worthy ancestors think that only men needed this facility after shop hours in Hitchin? There used to be a tiny gents urinal nestling in the wall at the foot of Windmill Hill; it was there until the mid 1970's.

In a century there have been ups and downs regarding the hill; whether to build on the top, what to build on the top, what to build at the bottom and what to do with the traffic, whether to keep the T junction with filters or whether to build a roundabout. As Hitchin folk come and go down the centuries, that hill will remain the lungs of the town.

Left: The Bancroft Players in a production of A Midsummer Night's Dream *at The Dell in 1951.*

Views of Windmill Hill. Right: The cluttered snow scene of the 1980s contrasts with the peaceful view of the 1950s below. Note the telephone box and gents' toilets on left.

QUEEN STREET

The end of Queen Street nearest to Bridge Street was known as Dead Street (due to the ravages of the Great Plague) until the mid nineteenth century. At the Walsworth Road end it was called Back Street, and as such, still existed in the 1880's. By 1856 Dead Street had become Queen Street, as a result of patriotic fervour, perhaps occasioned by Queen Victoria's brief visit to Hitchin Railway Station in 1850, or by the successful conclusion to the Crimean War in 1856. The street was also briefly known as Railway Street during the 1880's.

The insalubrious nature of the road also gave rise to the epithet 'The St Giles of Hitchin', according to Reginald Hine, the allusion being to the notorious criminal district of 18th century London.

Nowadays the name Queen Street refers to the road from Bridge Street to Hermitage Road, and includes St Mary's Square and the market area. The oldest buildings left standing are The British Schools (1857), The Bethel Chapel (1869) , The Lister House Hotel (circa 1880) and the terrace built by George Jeeves in 1875.

The area around Queen Street has seen a dramatic change during the twentieth century. It was once the most densely populated area in the town but now has only a few houses and two blocks of flats. It had some of the oldest buildings in the town but now has almost nothing earlier than the late 1800's. The major change came in the 1920's with the large scale slum clearance of the area in front of the church. The many yards, including Seymour's, Thorpe's, and the notorious Chapman's Yards, disappeared at this time. The street was known for the number of public houses along its length but all except the Bricklayer's Arms, rebuilt in 1922, and the Half Moon (now The Founders Inn) were demolished. Rose Craig (née Worbey) had her version of the ditty to remember their names:

'The *Old White Horse* hit the *Lion* and made the *Peacock* fly.

Turn the *Bushel* (and Strike) upside down and drink the *Two Brewers* dry.

King William said to *Robin Hood* fetch my *Peahen*

And give the *Bricklayers* (Arms) the The *Shoulder of Mutton*'

This group of cross-country runners, standing outside the (now) Lord Lister Hotel, were photographed in the early 1920's.

ESTABLISHED OVER A CENTURY.

John R. Brownlow,
(LATE WALKER),
Wholesale & Family BUTCHER.

Families supplied upon reasonable terms with

HOME-KILLED
English and Scotch Beef and Mutton,
DAIRY FED PORK,
ONLY OF THE FINEST QUALITY.

PRIME PICKLED TONGUES AND BEEF.
POSITIVELY the CHEAPEST HOUSE in the NEIGHBOURHOOD.

Queen Street, Hitchin.

Top: A 1930s photograph of Landlord William Barnard with his dog Prince. Note the cigarette machine and the Belisha Beacon.
Above: Advertisement from an early Hitchin Directory. The animals were slaughtered on the premises.
Right: A stalwart of the Licensed Victuallers' Association, Elizabeth Barnard ran the pub for almost forty years from 1929.

She said she could remember the names but never went inside!

Many businesses disappeared, including Lucas the baker, Stratton the barber and taxidermist and Mrs Kitchener's sweet shop, and also the Union Jack Club and the Girls' Club run by Miss Aillie Latchmore. One business which continued until the 1960's was the pie factory of W B Moss & Sons. Appetising smells pervaded the air whilst you waited for the Greenline bus on St Mary's Square. The Square was created around 1930 but later in the 1930's it was dug up close to the river to provide air raid shelters. Large areas remained derelict following the slum clearance or had temporary uses such as the land on the north side of Hollow Lane where the market stalls were stored between market days. The removal of the stalls and all rubbish from St Mary's Square, where the market had been relocated during the Second World War, were swiftly organised for many years with almost military precision by Bert Slingsby and his staff.

The land on the south side of Hollow Lane was used as a storage depot by the Third Tank Regiment during the Second World War and became the site of the new Telephone Exchange which opened in 1955. This was next door to the Bricklayer's Arms which was run for almost forty years by Elizabeth Barnard who took over the licence, together with her husband William, from George Cherry in 1929. She was an enthusiastic member of Hitchin Licensed Victuallers (and can be seen pouring a glass of beer in the photo). Her daughter Gladys (later Bradford-Best) worked in the office of the Hitchin Laundry when she first left school. The laundry had been established on the site at the end of the nineteenth century and had been known as the Hitchin Steam Laundry or the Hitchin Sanitary Laundry. It later became known as the Innisfail Laundry and finally closed for business in 1995. One member of the staff, Gladys Dellar, had worked at the laundry for almost sixty years. You can see the laundry site in the aerial photograph together with Thomson's Garage next door. Neil

Above: Photograph of Jill Grey taken in the early 1980's.
Below: Class 3 of the Girl's Section of the British Schools, taken around 1910.

The Jill Grey Collection

A hobby that started by accident is how Jill described it. The hobby became a passion and over a period of twenty-five years she collected material relating to the history of elementary education and the social history of children. There are in total thirty-four thousand items.

Jill moved to Hitchin after her marriage at the end of the Second World War. She had been interested in antique books in general but not in children's books until 1962 when she bought a Victorian Alphabet Book in a jumble sale. She then started to read up about children's literature. A year later she made an important discovery.

She was in Stevenage looking for antiques and she spotted a pile of books in the corner of a shop. The first one she picked up was The Governess by Sarah Fielding, dated 1749, it turned out to be the first edition – confirmed by the British Museum who only had the second! The Governess was an important book because it is the earliest original story book written for children and was the prototype of the school story.

Jill spent several years doing further research and locating other editions. In 1968 Oxford University Press published a facsimile edition using Jill's copy and for which she wrote an eighty-two page introduction and bibliography. Jill now started collecting seriously and travelled extensively around the country visiting friends and family - and every bookshop and antique shop in the vicinity.

It was Jill's wish that the British Schools buildings became a Historical Schools Museum. Sadly she died in 1987 before her wish could be realised. How happy she would have been to see the progress being made by Benchmark (the name chosen by the Hitchin British Schools Trust for the Museum site) and the people of Hitchin under the name of Friends of the British Schools Museum.

Welcome
to

BRITISH SCHOOLS

Operation
BENCHMARK
*- help us
to preserve
our heritage*

Thomson tells that his father bought the buildings and moved his business from Walsworth Road in 1934. Previously John Caines had run a motor coach and removal business from these premises. His 'White Heather' and 'White Rose' coaches were a familiar sight in the town. There was also the coachworks of G W Lawrence who advertised 'Highest Testimonials from well-known County People, titled and others' and the forge run by E A Males of Charlton.

Some of the garage buildings were rebuilt in 1947 after a fire and major rebuilding took place in 1970. The pair of houses next door, known as West View and Titmore Cottage, were built by the respected local builder Jeeves and was the site of his original yard before he moved further along the street to number 40. On the opposite side of the road was the butchers shop owned by John Brownlow. He had his own slaughter house and Ethel Barnard (later Manning) can remember hearing the squeals of the animals, and trying to peer in through the gates on her way to school. He was a very public-spirited man and was responsible for the provision of a pedestrian crossing outside his shop. Further

along Queen Street was Hitchin's first swimming pool which was fed directly from the River Hiz. The water was changed once a week and many people can still remember that the cold crystal clear spring water became luke warm and pea-green by the end of the week. The entrance can still be seen and is the left-hand of the two pedestrian brick archways of the so-called waterworks house. The row of three substantial houses in front of the former swimming pool were another Jeeves development and have attractive patterned terra-cotta tiles incorporated on the facade.

Perhaps the most significant building remaining in Queen Street is the British Schools soon to become a National Museum of Education. The school was founded in 1810 but the oldest surviving building is the unique Lancasterian school room built in 1837 to facilitate the monitorial teaching system. The buildings to provide a girls' school that fronts onto Queen Street were added in 1858. The significance of the site was realised in the 1970's by Jill Grey who displayed part of her vast collection of educational memorabilia in one of the classrooms when the buildings became an annexe of North Herts College. She

Left: The terra-cotta tiles adorn the houses built by George Jeeves in 1874, at 66/68 Queen Street. They were intended for his own children and constructed to a high standard.
Above: Doris, Beatie and Ruby Howard enjoying themselves at the Queen Street swimming baths in June 1928.

The Queen Street Laundry, later to become the Innisfail Laundry.
Left: Employees photographed before closure in April 1995.
Centre: Advertisement from Handbook to Hitchin 1897.
Bottom: The Press Room, 1961.

WE beg to point out that this article, being fragile, dropped in the process of cleaning. We think you will agree it is too worn to repair successfully.

SANITARY STEAM LAUNDRY.

33 Queen Street, Hitchin.

Fitted with the Latest Improvements.

Inspection Invited.   Price Lists on application.

also arranged for the buildings to be listed. Ethel Barnard can remember an incident shortly after her little sister Joyce joined her at the British School. The infamous rampaging cattle entered the school yard and all the children ran to find safety. The quick thinking of one of the teachers, one of the Miss Days, resulted in Joyce being placed in an empty dustbin with the lid firmly in place until danger had passed. Stephen Bradford-Best can remember the urinal built into the retaining wall in the corner of the school yard which is now bricked up. Will it be restored one day?

In addition to the Bethel Chapel, built in 1869, which remains, there was also the Congregational Church next door to the British Schools. The site was redeveloped by John Willmott & Sons in the 1970's when they transferred their headquarters there from Walsworth Road. It was subsequently occupied by Gardner Merchant Ltd., the contract caterers. The pair of houses opposite may have been saved had the original plan to provide underground parking at the new garage next door been possible. One of the houses was the manse to the church and the other the laundry manager's house occupied in its last years by Bob Adams. Next door was the garage of E A Prime who also had a garage in Ashwell. Edward Prime bought the site from the Tooley's and moved into Chestnut House with his wife and family. The house was built with

Fine buff coloured square chimney pots with spiked tops.

the best materials and included Italian marble fireplaces and a mahogany staircase. In addition to the workshops and car showroom, a large garage was leased to the Eastern National Bus Company until they moved to their new garage in Fishponds Road. Edward Prime was a keen motorist and campaigned his 1913 Fiat in reliability trials well into the 1930's. This car is now in the National Motor Museum at Beaulieu. Following his sudden death during the Second World War the business was run by his daughter Molly Wilson until it was sold to H A Saunders Ltd. They also bought other property to enable them to build a large garage and move their business from Brand Street (where Sainsbury's now stands). The other properties purchased included the Hillview Hotel around the corner at the end of Bridge Street, formerly known as the Triangle. On the corner had been the veterinary surgery of Goldsmith, previously Kendall, but the building was demolished by a bus in 1951! The excavations for the underground car park on the large site of the new garage were thwarted by water rapidly filling the trenches. Instead the site was expanded to provide street level parking by the purchase and demolition of the two houses mentioned earlier. Opposite the garage, where Cannon House now stands, were the earliest buildings to survive to the later twentieth century and included Ship Yard and Davies Alley. Various businesses were also based there, including Grant the builder, Frank West the carpenter and undertaker and ending with the Half Moon public house (now The Found Inn). The row of buildings were demolished in the 1950's, some dating back to the reign of the first Queen Elizabeth. Would they be preserved if they survived today? There can be no doubt that the changes have been dramatic but may have been even more so if a major widening scheme in the 1960's had been given the go-ahead. This would have resulted in some properties, such as the row of three splendid Jeeves' houses, being left on a dual carriageway traffic island. Fortunately the scheme was abandoned largely because of a well-organised campaign co-ordinated by one of the residents, Miss Aughton.

Above: Scarcely recognisable today, both the cottages in Queen Street (on the right) and behind The Triangle have gone.

Below: A well turned-out Cycling Club pose in front of the Kirklands Hotel, supported by interested local residents.

BRIDGE STREET

Bridge Street takes its name from the bridge over the River Hiz, originally the site of a ford. The present bridge was built in 1784 (notice the date stone). In the years before the bridge was built the street was known as Spittle Street, after the hospital and pest house which once stood near here, then one of the unhealthiest regions of the town.

Facing the Lord Lister Hotel is the area known as The Triangle. Where the mini-roundabout is now located, there was once a fine group of acacia trees surrounded by iron

Lucas Brewery

The modern Crown House occupies part of the site of Hitchin's most ancient brewery, that of the Lucases. It was founded in 1709 to utilise locally grown barley, a crop which contributed to Hitchin's prosperity. Early on in its history the Lucases, who were Quakers, were in partnership with a brother-in-law, one Isaac Gray, but eventually they took over completely. Their premises, on the corner of Angel Street (now Sun Street) and Bridge Street remained on the same site for the whole of the firm's lifetime.

The firm became a limited company in 1896 but after the death of Samuel Lucas the younger in 1919 the brewery suffered from increased labour costs, post war inflation and the very dry weather of the early 1920's which may well have caused insuperable problems to a process which relied heavily on water. The business was bought by the Luton brewery company of J W Green Ltd in 1920 but was closed three years later. The buildings were finally demolished in 1963. Green's themselves later merged with Flower & Sons Ltd of Stratford-on-Avon and Flower's subsequently were taken over by Whitbread & Company Ltd.

In its hey-day Lucases made Bridge Street one of the sweetest smelling streets in the town and they became renowned for their generous Harvest Home suppers held in the Maltings.

In Victorian times, bottles containing beer and mineral water were made of different coloured glass and came in a wide variety of shapes.
Far left: Transfer-printed stone bottle for ginger beer, sealed with a cork.
Centre: A flat-bottomed Hamilton bottle, made before 1872.
Near left: Mineral water bottle designed by Hiram Codd.

railings and, beyond them, a row of old cottages where Mann Egerton recently stood. Opposite is the garage, built about 1930, which, for many years, housed Hitchin's London Transport buses.

Further along is Mr Eric Moore's bookshop. Built in 1830 as two cottages, it very soon became yet another public house, The Postboy, so called after the first landlord's former occupation. Here can be seen a board commemorating George Chapman.

Number 28 was built in the late nineteenth

Bridge Street, Hitchin.   *J Burwell, A.R.C.A.*

Above: Bridge Street, as depicted in one of a series of woodcut illustrations produced as postcards by the Bancroft Press.

Above: Advertisement from HUDC Guide 1910.
Left: Label used on brown beer bottles between 1896 and 1923.

century as Odell's carriage works. Odell's originally built and maintained horsedrawn vehicles but they also began to build bodies for the early motor cars. Beyond number 28 is a building which formerly housed The Boot, a public house dating from about 1800. Tradition has it that soldiers were billeted here in 1803, during an invasion scare in the Napoleonic War.

Standing on the bridge you can see the manhole in the river. Although a modern one, it reminds us that Hitchin became one of the first towns to take advantage of the 1848 Public Health Act. A main sewer was built to run under the river bed itself.

Transport In Hitchin
late 40s - 50s

Derek Larkins recalls that Birch Brothers operated a very popular coach service from Rushden Northants to London Kings Cross and return every hour seven days a week. Thousands of RAF personnel were transported from local RAF stations into Hitchin and Kings Cross. Huge six wheel and heavy double deck coaches always travelled spot on time. These coaches travelled into Hitchin via Blakes Corner, Bancroft and out via Sun Street and Bridge Street. The latest coaches were built for the Festival of Britain in 1951 and were called the 'Marlborough'. Each coach was called after the House of Marlborough for instance 'Winston Churchill' etc. You will see from the photographs that the coaches were massive, over fifteen feet high and more than eight feet wide, very safe to drive and comfortable for the passengers. After leaving the stop opposite Woolworth's for London, drivers had not only to negotiate the old market square but line their coaches up to pass in between Curry's and the Angel Public House. They had to be careful to miss the overhanging shop and pub signs, inches were very important, then down into Sun Street where it was more than possible they would meet other Birch Bros. coaches coming into Hitchin from London. Passengers could look down from the top deck into the bedroom windows. I was on my way to work one morning and talking to the milkman when all of a sudden just behind us the old Angel pub fell down, we were both lucky not to

Right: Market Square circa 1922.
Below: Bus ticket issued in exchange for a return ticket. Destinations were punched.

have been under it. If the service coach started to fill up the conductor or an inspector would telephone control and immediately the manager, Mr (Paddy) Walsh, would send out stand-by crews with a spare coach. A local service to Whitwell and Holwell was also run by Birch Bros. From driving with Birch Bros I then started on London Transport working from the LT garage in Bridge Street. London Transport also ran an hourly service from Hitchin St Mary's Square to London and Chertsey called the 716. This was an excellent service starting at 6 am every day of the week and on every hour until 9 pm. The coach and bus garage is now 22 Bridge Street. Inside this garage was a complete workshop, offices etc. The shop in Bridge Street, now Eric Moore's Book Shop, was the staff canteen. In the summer time drivers had to wear 'Pudding Cloths' on their hats (a white cloth) and could only remove jackets when a notice was put up and then only on condition that no braces were shown.

Above: Coach driver Mr Walker and his conductor about to start on their seven-and-a-half hour return journey to Chertsey.

Above: A nine-and-a-half ton Marlborough bus, made especially for Birch Bros. for service between Rushden and Kings Cross.
Above right: The drivers as named on the photograph wait for orders while on relief duty.
Bottom right: Advertisement in 1951 Pageant Souvenir Programme.

TILEHOUSE STREET

In 1941 Reginald L Hine, Hitchin's famous historian, described Tilehouse Street as the most fascinating and attractive of all our town's streets. That fascination, of its six hundred year span of local history, survives today.

'Tylehousestret', first mentioned by name in the Court of Rolls of 1460, formed the south-west boundary of medieval Hitchin. Originally the area between the street and Bancroft was an open market, already thriving by the late thirteenth century. Gradually its stalls were replaced by permanent buildings to form present day Bucklersbury and Sun Street. From its earliest years Tilehouse Street probably possessed a mixture of business and residential properties and its varied character is alive in present day Hitchin.

The form of the street also dates from its very earliest years, in fact many of the buildings probably contain elements of medieval timber framed construction, although this is not always obvious from their present appearance. 'Modernisation' was just as common in the past as today and this is why what we see is not always exactly what it seems.

Before Barham's, Sun Street joins at the point where Tilehouse and Bridge Streets meet. Traditionally this was the site of the annual May celebrations complete with pole. Opposite the junction is the rear of the Priory, for years the home of the Delmé-Radcliffes. The original line of the road to Charlton, called Mill Lane after the malt mills located near here, runs between the Priory pond and Number 1 Tilehouse Street. The diversity of roof levels, building lines, chimneys, materials and colour can all be seen as you look along the street.

The black weather-boarded shop on the right (No 95) is Barham's gun shop. This late medieval building has a continuous jetty and crown post roof and was once an important part of the Hitchin textile trade, the source of much local wealth. The Papworths, a wool stapling family, used it as a wool store and, much later, Mr Barker made tweeds here. The premises of Francis Newton were at Numbers 93 and 94.

Francis Newton – Builder

The building firm of Francis Newton could lay strong claim to be the oldest building company in Hitchin. The firm was founded some time before 1676 by members of the Coulson family. About one hundred years later John Coulson apprenticed his nephew Robert Newton for seven years. On John Coulson's death Robert Newton took over the business and ran it under his own name. The years went by and in 1810 he took his son Isaac into partnership and the firm continued under the style Newton & Son, Painters, Plumbers & Glaziers.

Issac Newton continued to run the business after his father's death in 1836 and he became increasingly involved with the running of the town's fire brigade. Isaac Newton himself died in 1859, to be succeeded by his son Thomas, who married into the Gatward family, but his son Francis nearly disrupted the family association with the business for, after his apprenticeship in Hertford and a brief spell in Bedford, he almost resolved not to work in Hitchin and then thought better of it.

Francis Newton went into partnership with his brother Edgar for several years, and the business expanded until it had more than three hundred employees. Francis Newton was responsible for many improvements to Hitchin's water supply and sewage disposal systems. He died in 1922 and the business then suffered something of a decline in the hands of his sons Basil and George, but five years later two employees, Harry Day and Tom Coleman bought the firm. They continued until their deaths, both in 1952, when Harry Day's son Philip took charge. The business

Hitchin, Tilehouse Street.

*Above: Tilehouse Street before
the First World War.
Below: Newton's the Builders,
with their crane, right, still to
be seen in Tilehouse Street.
Drawn by Clarissa Szirtes.*

*Above: The Cooper's Arms
drawn by Clarissa Szirtes.*

Paeckmeyer connections with Newton's over Four Generations

Four generations of Paeckmeyer have their initials in the lead on the roof of St Mary's Church.

Gilliam Paeckmeyer was a Belgian, injured at the Battle of the Somme and sent to Cambridge to recover, met and married a nurse. He had to go back to Belgium for two years after the First World War to help repair war damage and returned to this country in 1920 and worked for Francis Newton.

Maurice Paeckmeyer, his son, was apprenticed to Francis Newton in 1938, aged fourteen, retired in 1989.

Glenn Paeckmeyer, Maurice's son, was apprenticed there in 1962.

Michael Paeckmayer, Glenn's son, was 'loaned' to Francis Newton in 1989 and went up on St Mary's roof with his grandfather Maurice.

Through connections with Francis Newton they have all worked on various properties in the area.

---

remained in Tilehouse Street until 1994. Matthew Day now runs the firm from Ickleford. There is a connection between the Newton families and Sir Isaac Newton.

Over the years the Newton Company became involved in a great variety of projects, from repairs to St Mary's Church between 1775 and 1909, which bear dated inscriptions, to construction and repair of many houses covering a wide area.

Number 3 is another medieval timber building with jettying and still exhibits herringbone pargetting. It was once the Wheatsheaf Inn and, because it had no

Rare early photograph taken in The Cooper's Arms yard. Dovecotes were not only decorative as the eggs were collected and consumed. From a scrapbook compiled by George Aylott in the 1880s. Below: Footscraper in Tilehouse Street drawn by Becky Hull.

Hitchin Cream

Hitchin Cream was the name of a sherry specially shipped by the Hertford brewers, McMullen & Sons. The product belonged to G B Christie Ltd, who were wine and spirit merchants at 3 Bancroft, having been taken over years ago by McMullens. The sherry was introduced in 1951 for the Festival of Britain and production ceased about 1983.

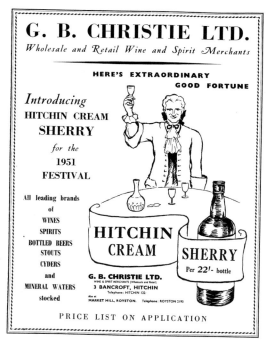

G. B. CHRISTIE LTD.

Wholesale and Retail Wine and Spirit Merchants

HERE'S EXTRAORDINARY GOOD FORTUNE

Introducing
HITCHIN CREAM
SHERRY
for the
1951 FESTIVAL

All leading brands
of
WINES
SPIRITS
BOTTLED BEERS
STOUTS
CYDERS
and
MINERAL WATERS
stocked

HITCHIN CREAM

SHERRY
Per 22/- bottle

G. B. CHRISTIE LTD.
WINE & SPIRIT MERCHANTS (Wholesale and Retail)
3 BANCROFT, HITCHIN
Telephone: HITCHIN 122.
Also at
MARKET HILL, ROYSTON. Telephone: ROYSTON 2193

PRICE LIST ON APPLICATION

Above: Unusual wooden corkscrew advertising 'local' sherry!
Right: Advertisement in the Hitchin Pageant Souvenir programme 1951.

carriageway, horses had to be led through the bar parlour to the rear stables! Hitchin's first telephone exchange was housed in this row.

Numbers 83 and 84 are both eighteenth century brick built houses, though number 84 acquired an extra storey later. One late nineteenth century occupant, lawyer Frederick Wright, is said to have seen his brother in midshipman's uniform standing by his bed a few days before news of his ship's loss reached Hitchin.

The Cooper's Arms (Numbers 81-82), is one of the most interesting buildings in the street. The structure of the Cooper's Arms is of uncertain age but the tracery of some of the windows is reminiscent of an ecclesiastical style. It is also said to have been the Tylers' (brickmakers) or Woolstaplers' Guildhall, but it may simply have been the house of a wealthy resident. In 1832 the buildings were described as 'Ancient Houses' and it is 1860 before any reference to a public house is found. McMullen's bought the Cooper's Arms in 1887 for £900 after the death of Jack Webb, 'beer retailer and fly proprietor' when it was described as:

'...prominently situated in Tilehouse Street, Hitchin, and doing excellent trade, containing conveniently arranged bar, bar room, tap room, living room, kitchen, five good bedrooms and two cellars in basement with extensive business premises at the rear comprising three stables, chaise house, cart sheds, two large barns, storehouse, piggeries, fowl house, coal and wood barns, granary and cowshed and numerous other erections' all for £50 per year'.

Samuel Lucas

Samuel Lucas was born in 1805 at The Tile House (now numbers 25, 26 and 27) in Tilehouse Street, the second son of William Lucas, the owner of Hitchin's brewery and a prominent Quaker in the town. He was educated at Hitchin Free School, the forerunner of the Boys' Grammar School and later at the Society of Friends School near Bristol. It was at the latter place of learning that he developed his love of sketching and drawing, this father could not approve of this practice.

When he was fourteen he was apprenticed to a shipowner and wharfinger at Southwick and subsequently to a Wapping corn merchant. It was while he was working by the River Thames that he pursued his pastime of painting with the utmost vigour, but only in the evening when business was finished for the day.

Plaque on the wall of a carriage entrance.

In 1825 his father relented when he wrote: 'I am willing so far to patronise the arts, as to engage to take off thy hands anything, whether it be in oils or water colours, on thine own terms'. Samuel exhibited an oil painting of a sea scene at the Royal Academy in 1828. Six years later he returned to Hitchin to work at the family brewery. In 1837 he married and in 1844 he frequently exhibited his pictures. The death of his wife in 1849 was a great shock to him and he distracted himself in the work of the brewery and the local parish.

Samuel Lucas married for a second time in 1862 and his wife encouraged him to take up art again and he executed many pen and ink sketches. A mild stroke three years later made painting difficult and he died, in the room in which he was born, in 1870.

Above left: A Hitchin Scold.
Above right: A Hitchin Drover. Two of many sketches by Samuel Lucas to be found in Reginald Hine's books.

Right: Hitchin Memorial Garden, drawn by Clarissa Szirtes.

The house (number 12) recorded in the sale's particulars was occupied by the Day family of basket makers around 1880 and it remained their shop until Mr George Day died about 1955.

The Three Tuns

The pub (number 11) has had many owners. In 1817 William Smith had his licence suspended for irregular conduct. Other publicans include Daniel Baldock in 1801, Sam Bradley in 1830, George Bailey in 1851, George Taylor in 1880 Edward Day in 1899, James Sharp in 1910 and Robert Burns in 1922. An old Hitchin legend suggested that if a man stumbled going up the steps at the entrance he would not get served.

The pub contained three downstairs rooms which were a tap room, a kitchen and a wash house all with flagstone floors, plus a large

At the far end of the street is situated the Hine Memorial Garden. Since the Priory bypass was opened in 1981, the Garden has formed the westernmost end of Lower Tilehouse Street. Dedicated in September 1952, it is a fitting tribute to Reginald Hine (1883 - 1949) who lavished so much time and affection on Hitchin's past. A plaque bears the inscription:

'Semper in Libris Praebuit Speculum Mundi':

'In his books he supplied a mirror of the world'.

Appropriately the Garden stands on the site of Hitchin's Free School, founded in 1639 by John Mattocke in an old house '. . . which time beyond memory of man had been used for a schoolehouse for the education of the children of the inhabitants of Hitchin'. The school survived here until 1876. The building remained until 1949 when it fell victim to a road improvement scheme. The school foundation stone is set in the Garden wall.

little drain in the floor where the beer could drain away. After its closure the pub became a newsagents for Mr & Mrs Harding.

By 1982 restoration work was being done by brothers Peter and Duncan Wilshere who exposed all the wattle and daub walls. It is now a beautifully restored home owned by Mr & Mrs Stephenson who have lived there since August 1988. There have been some special finds by the present occupants. In the back yard various bits of clay pipes have been found and some slipware (pottery) which is brown with yellow splotches on it.

The seasonal farm workers who came to the town from Scotland and Ireland provided a story here. Reginald Hine tells how these people had swarmed into the town to break up the worship at Tilehouse Street Baptist Chapel, tossing a sheep's head through the open window to annoy the congregation. This happened to such good effect that when the worshippers heard a coarse voice shout 'There's turnips to follow', they rushed out and chased the perpetrator down the hill. He wisely hid in a cornbin at the Three Tuns until the hunt went by. 'Otherwise', he declared, 'I should have been dipped for a Baptist in the Priory horse pond'.

In number 23 lived Charles Times, whose son, William Onslow Times (1851 - 1934), became 'the father' of Hitchin's local government.

The Three Tuns drawn by Clarissa Szirtes

cellar. It also had three good bedrooms and a large attic with window at floor level. There was stabling for twelve horses, several barns and a wood yard.

The pub was closed in 1923 but it still has some impressive features, for example, the beautiful central carriageway and the original door on the right-hand side of the house. Behind this is a part of the cellar where the barrels of beer were stored. There is also a

OLD PARK ROAD

The 1844 map of the area shows the beginning of housing development on the west side of the road, with blocks of cottages and yards starting to front the pasture land and allotment gardens that characterised this still largely rural route in and out of the town. The Tilehouse Street end was closely packed with small houses occupied by 'various tenants', the Waggon & Horses Public House originally being part of a row built at the end of the eighteenth century. It opened in the early 1840's as a beer house, and is remembered for its open door, presumably to attract both light and custom to the gloomy bar area. This hostelry was later to witness the accidental death of a drunken reveller. A policeman summoned to a scuffle outside the premises, subdued a miscreant by kneeling on his stomach, an action which brought about his death.

From the middle of the nineteenth century a mixture of housing occupied this side of the road. Some substantially built, were lived in by owner occupiers. Blocks of cottages, some poorly constructed, were let to tenants. Halfway down, the Horse & Jockey Public House was built by the banker Joseph Margetts Pierson, and opened in 1846. Unusually it had a mainly chalk block construction. It was demolished in 1990 its place has been taken by a new conveyor carwash belonging to Burrs.

Numbers 22 and 22a Old Park Road became the office and yard for C F Burr & Sons, Builders. Later this became Willmotts and finally Silvertons, Builders Merchants & Hardware Dealers. Number 23 was a substantial property occupied by Dr H R Grellett and his family from the 1920's until 1948. A room at the front of the house was used as a surgery and the grounds extended back as far as Westfield Lane. Pansy Wells (Mrs Pansy Mitchell) remembers watching Dr Grellett's daughters playing tennis on their court from the back bedroom window in Taylor's Cottages. Subsequently the house was used by a Charitable Trust; Burr's premises expanded, the house was demolished in 1966 and 1967 saw the establishment of Burr Bros 'Hitchin Service Station'. A rare and beautiful beech tree in the grounds was protected by a preservation order. Its presence later determined the layout of the garage premises. Sadly the tree died!

Tucked behind this area of Old Park Road were Taylors Cottages, built in the 1840's, and vividly remembered by Pansy Mitchell who was born at Number 6. Despite the sometimes difficult conditions she has happy memories of a caring and supportive group of neighbours. 'A row of seven cottages, two rooms up and two down with only a front door. A single tap outside provided the water and the toilets were at the bottom of the gardens. The right of way to these cottages was through a passage from Old Park Road.

These cottages were built on the site of an old barn and had lathe and plaster walls with slate roofs. They were lit by gas and had old kitchen coppers. On Sunday evenings the coppers were filled with water and the fires laid underneath. Monday was wash day and we all had cold food on a Monday as the women did not have time to cook. It was hard work scrubbing shirt collars and boiling the sheets etc. Then all the dirty water had to be taken out of the coppers and tipped down the drain outside. Life was very hard especially in the winter when the water tap was frozen, to say nothing of the toilets! I think the thing I remember most was having a bath on a Saturday night. We had a long zinc bath and it was placed in front of the fire in the front room. A real luxury in such primitive conditions. Early memories also include the necessity of opening the front door to sweep out the water which percolated through the walls during torrential rain. The cottages were

Top: Waggon and Horses prior to demolition in 1981.
Far left: Unusually located hydrant marker above doorway.
Near left: Victorian post-box.
Below: Wall-mounted footscraper drawn by Becky Hull.

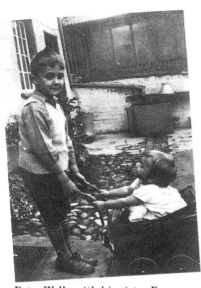

Peter Wells with his sister Pansy in her doll's pram, 1935.

Taylors Cottages, Old Park Road.

Mrs Day, with Mr and Mrs Hagger and their son.

condemned by the council before the Second World War, although the occupants were not re-housed until the early 1950's'.

At the end of the road at Numbers 66/67 stands former shop premises with a Benchmark cut into the wall and Hitchin's only surviving Victorian post box set into the face. Robert Walmsley remembers the end shop as the little barber's shop of John Chambers, '. . . a football team supporter all his life and an old Hitchin character'. Pansy Mitchell remembers the shop next to the hairdresser's being run as a sweet shop during the Second World War by Miss Crawley. 'She sold raw carrots which had been soaked in sugar water. . . they were half-a-penny each'. Near the shop in the middle of the road at its junction with Bedford Road and Union Road (now Oughtonhead Way), stood a fountain. Under a big street lamp was a drinking trough for horses with a smaller one for dogs set below.

On the town side of Old Park Road development was much slower. The map of 1844 shows a continuous expanse of pasture land. Home Close was glebeland and further down Salters Dell was owned by Charles

Wilshere. The 1898 map shows the situation still largely unchanged, but Hitchin was expanding. In the thirty years following the 1891 Census the population was to increase by one third. In 1903 the new sheep, pig and beef market in the Lairage was laid out at a cost of £2000. The bustle of commerce was moving closer! However a stile and path still gave access to pasture land at Nuns Close and until the early years of the century this side of the road comprised unmetalled footpath and hedgerows. Soon afterwards a row of villas was to be erected. Pansy Mitchell recalls that her grandfather refused to build near the junction of Old Park Road and Nuns Close. It had been the site of an old gravel pit, although subsequently filled in by rubbish. His hunch proved correct as the house erected later was plagued by subsidence.

Mr Blood, the Town Surveyor responsible for much of the early housing at Sunnyside and Westmill, lived at the house opposite Number 23 (now the dentists). It was built in 1904. Crabbs Close and North End, both detached properties, have now been demolished, their places taken by the supermarket car park and flats.

Smithson's Recreation Ground

'The use of this open space is restricted to women and children (boys up to the age of five years only)'.

Hitchin Official Guide 1968

The history of this recreation ground is arguably the most interesting of any in the town. It was given by Mrs Sarah Smithson (1844 - 1928) in memory of her husband, Edward. He was a solicitor who committed suicide in 1920. His wife, a member of the Society for Psychial Research, sought the help of a medium and through him her spouse expressed his wish to have a meadow near their home turned into a public recreation ground. Two of her conditions of use were that access was to be limited to women and girls and boys under the age of five years and that before a band was allowed to play permission had to be sought from the occupiers of the neighboring cottages (now the site of the new Court House in Old Park Road). This proposal was the first of its kind in England and was approved by the Ministry of Health in 1926. However the Sex Discrimination Act 1974/5 laid down that such a bye-law could not take precedence over national law and the recreation ground is now open to all. As a result, a large wooden sign giving details of the restriction on use had to be taken away. Also lost due to road widening was a large landmark in the shape of a Cedar of Lebanon, popularly known as the 'umbrella tree'.

In 1994 the recreation ground was updated to make the play area safer and more interesting for children. The new surface is made by the 'wet pore' process which uses recycled lorry tyre treads; colours are added to give children a visual guide.

A charming photograph of Mrs Smithson.

The 'New Recreation Ground' in the late 1920s.

WEST HILL

With the new century, enterprise and expansion blossomed in Old Park Road! In 1904 Francis John Wells (Frank) a Master Builder, came to live with his family at Number 37. He had been an apprentice to Walter Jeeves in Queen Street. In 1906 he bought the three adjacent cottages and in their demolition he opened up an entrance for a new road on land owned by William Onslow Times. Plots were sold off to individual buyers who then had houses built. Many of these were built by Frank Wells himself. A typical plot cost £120. Restrictive Covenants ensured that a single dwelling should cost not less than £400 and a pair not less than £700. Only 'genteel professions' could be carried out on the premises and a five foot wall or close boarded fence had to separate each property!

By 1920 twenty houses had been built and with names like 'The Laurels' and 'The Beeches'; only Number 4 admitted to a street number! One of the earliest purchasers was Superintendant John Reynolds, the Deputy Chief Constable of Hertfordshire, who retired from the force in 1911 but who lived out a long and active retirement at 'Bramfield' (now number 30). Early development stopped at the line of the footpaths to Westfield and Gaping Lanes, but 'the Extension' as it was known, continued after the First World War and by 1940 ninety eight houses had been built.

Francis John Wells himself continued to live and work at Number 37 Old Park Road. Following the demolition of the cottages next to his house, he rebuilt his side wall adding a loft and extension.

Wells' Garage

While still a schoolboy Frank's son, Frank Herbert Wells (born in 1898) developed an interest in mechanics and worked part time at J McIntosh's garage in Exchange Yard. Leaving school in 1912 he worked briefly in the foundry and machine shop at Heatley & Gresham's, then at the Foster Instrument Co. Soon after joining Innes & Co in Walsworth Road the First World War broke out. Young Bert, as he was known, immediately volunteered by joining the Royal Naval Air Service. By February 1915 he was in France. By the age of nineteen he was placed in charge of a fleet of travelling workshops testing aeroplanes for pilots to take into service. Demobbed in 1919 he returned to McIntosh's garage until 1923. For some time young Bert had been using the loft at No 37 for 'odd jobs'. Demand for his services grew and in 1925 he and his father built the workshop and garage still standing in its original form at the bottom of West Hill. The walnut tree bears witness to its orchard garden site.

Bert Wells soon established a thriving business as he was a clever and innovative engineer. There was little he could not turn his hand to, from building tractors to inventing machinery for Kayser Bondor. Funfair proprietors, Thurston's used to rely on his skills to keep their roundabouts and side shows going. (His efforts were frequently rewarded with a fresh coconut!). Marrying in 1928 he settled his wife and family at Number 6 Taylors Cottages, next to the garage from where he ran his business.

Life here continued to provide incident. Following a particularly severe storm in the late 1950's the back wall of the row showed signs of detaching itself! Undaunted, Bert Wells sought the aid of Mr Deamer, the removal man, who helped Bert to push tie-bars through the far corner of Numbers 1 and 2. The Wells' furniture was then moved down from Number 6 and a new home was set up! Having bought the row of now derelict cottages, Bert eventually pulled them down and set about erecting a bungalow on the site. His daughter, Pansy, still lives there. He continued to run his business until 1980, when he died.

Left: 'Grampy' Wells with grandchildren Peter and Pansy and their replica Vauxhall car c1936.
Bottom left: Pansy serving petrol, 1946.
Main photograph: Looking towards Old Park Road, 1947. The walnut tree still stands.

A pleasing Edwardian doorway with original furniture.

Door from early years of the century. An unusual central lozenge design surrounded by glass panes.

Benchmarks

Locating and recording local benchmarks was a particular interest of the late Ben Ward. These incised symbols were usually cut on walls or kerbstones, giving the point of a precise measure of land above sea level made by the Ordnance Survey. On maps they are represented thus 'B. M. – 224.9', but on buildings themselves only the arrow pattern appears.

The arrow symbol was taken from the armorial bearings of an early chief of the Ordnance Department.

Sadly many of these marks are gradually disappearing due to property repairs or neglect.

This fine example can be found on the wall of No. 61. Using the recently published Ordnance Survey map reprint of Hitchin in 1898, readers will be able to trace others in the area.

Benchmark (224.9) on the wall of 61 Old Park Road.

THE HITCHIN CRICKET CLUB

'Hitchin Town Cricket Club, which has a ground in a remarkable scenic position on the summit of Gaping Hills, commanding a panoramic view over the surrounding country'

Hitchin Official Guide 1959/60

A SHORT HISTORY BY F A TROMANS

From a brochure used by Hitchin Cricket Club to support their tour of Barbados in 1993

Reginald Hine tells us that it was one of the members of the Radcliffe family who was responsible for founding the Hitchin Cricket Club. In 1866 he gathered a group of men who for some time had played single wicket matches on Butts Close, and provided them with a spacious ground on Hitchin Hill. The Club functioned there until 1925.

Within the first ten years the Club had many teething troubles but despite this in 1876 twenty four matches were played. There were three different membership subscriptions, each allowing the member differing privileges. For £1 he could play and practise and he and any other member of his family could drive or ride into the ground. For ten shillings he alone could drive or ride into the ground, five shillings allowed him access to the ground on foot only.

It was obvious that playing membership was confined to those Hitchin citizens who were socially acceptable. One and two day matches were the order of the day and in addition to the professional, a number of non-members whose prowess at cricket was accepted, were included in the teams. Attempts were made from time to time to rectify this state of affairs, but as late as 1909, in an anonymous letter to the local newspaper, a paid up member of the Club complained that the Club was run by a 'little family party' for the sole benefit of that 'family'! He went on to state that he had never been invited to play, and no attempt was ever made to discover his cricketing ability. The Committee wisely decided not to reply publicly, so maybe a sense of guilt was activated by the letter.

There were obviously stresses and strains in these early days, for in 1876, at a General Meeting, some of the members proposed that the Club be wound up, but after a long discussion this motion was defeated.

The selection of the team was not carried out in the normally accepted manner. Prior to the beginning of each season, managers were appointed to take complete charge of the various matches on the fixture list, and members wishing to play had to notify the selected manager three weeks before each game.

In 1880 the question of a pavilion was mooted and a Pavilion Fund opened with Mr S Tuke appointed as Treasurer. The response to the appeals must have been generous for in 1882 the wooden pavilion was built and erected by Mr Foster, at a cost of £85.

In 1882 serious attempts were made to widen the appeal of the Club and it was decided to play a number of Saturday afternoon games, to select only members of the Club to play in these games and to exclude professionals. But these remained laudable intentions and did not appear to bear fruit. A professional was engaged from the earliest years and he had to be available on three evenings each week at five o' clock to bowl to members, and on Saturdays to play in the matches. Umpires, scorers and gatekeepers were also paid. By 1886 the Honorary Secretary was despondent about the generally low standard of cricket played by the team, and in particular complained of the weakness of the bowling, primarily because too much reliance was placed on Wilson, the professional.

The Club's attitude to neighbouring clubs was autocratic, and matches with these clubs were mostly discontinued, because it was found to be almost impossible to make up an eleven to play away from home. So, in 1884, eighteen games were played at home and only one away, and the figures in 1892 were nineteen to six, after efforts had been made to change this attitude. However, the ground and facilities were very good indeed, and were said to be the envy of other clubs in the County. Consequently, it was easy to fill gaps in the fixture list by attracting good, strong wandering sides, which welcomed the opportunity to play under such good conditions. The Hertfordshire County Club regularly played County games on the ground, and in addition the ground was hired to stage some most attractive games. In fact the Club itself must have provided a feast of cricket for discerning cricketers, as this extract from the 1892 fixture list shows:

18th July   M C C
19/20th July I Zingari
21/22nd July Gents of Herts
2/3rd August Public Schools
22/23 August Hertfordshire v Lincolnshire.

The ground was also used for tennis, but relations with the Tennis Club were far from satisfactory, and in 1897 it ceased to function. North Herts Hockey Club also rented the ground for several seasons, and at one stage permission was granted for two Rugby Football matches to be played here. These extra games, together with the Annual Athletics Sports, a great local attraction run by the Cricket Club for a few years, meant that the ground was used throughout the year.

The Club ceased to function during the First World War, and when it was restarted it was obvious that interest and membership had widened, and that the Club was becoming more democratic.

Half day matches were arranged, the team was selected by a constitutionally elected selection committee, and fixtures were arranged for a second XI; but in 1925 the Club received a shattering blow, for its lovely ground was swallowed up in the relentless quest for suitable building land for an expanding town. The Club, with whom such well known citizens as the brothers Wright and Grellet, F Passingham, F R Shillitoe, G Smyth, Guy Gainsford, H Williams, R Hine, F

Coxall and A H Foster had been so closely associated, had now to seek pastures new.

Eventually a ground adjoining the London Road, at the end of the Longbridge Estate, between Hitchin and St Ippollyts was rented from the Headmaster of Caldicott School and cricket was played here for the next thirteen years. Thanks to the efforts of stalwarts like Sid Brown, the professional, the pavilion and 'square' were transported to the new ground and cricket began once again.

In 1938 Caldicott School moved to a new home in Buckinghamshire and the Club had to decide whether to buy the ground or vacate it. War clouds were gathering and the decision was made to move to the newly opened King George V Playing Field in Bedford Road, after suitable arrangements had been made with the Hitchin U D C. Once again the 'square' and pavilion were moved though this place was obviously not suitable as a permanent home. The game was kept alive during the war years by a small band of stalwarts, who had to deal with obstacles and difficulties which would have daunted any but the most persistent. During this time Mr Harry Russell, who had headed the team's batting and bowling averages in 1910, was determined that the Club should have a permanent home worthy of its name and tradition, was busy looking for a suitable ground. His vision and enthusiasm proved infectious, and with the support of such men as Mr J Rivett, Mr A King, Mr C F Coxall, Mr C J Widdows, Mr G Smyth and Mr F R Shillitoe a suitable home was found. It was thanks to the generosity of Mr Hubert and Mr Wallace Moss that it became possible to purchase the present ground at Lucas Lane. A non-profit making company, The Hitchin Cricket Ground Ltd. , was formed to take care of the financial position and future of the ground. The Directors were all friends and patrons of the Club and it was their responsibility to ensure that, in accordance with the Moss brothers' wishes, the ground was used for cricket in perpetuity. The Company leased the ground to the Cricket Club so that at last it was assured of a ground which it could claim as its own.

But there was still much to be done. A rough field had to be transformed into a cricket ground and this was done with a zest which augured well for the future. The disused Isolation Hospital nearby was purchased, transported and erected to form a spacious and most suitable pavilion; turf was brought from Butts Close to form the 'square' and by 1947 the ground was ready for the specially arranged opening game. With such facilities the Club went from strength to strength. Two teams were fielded each week and Sunday cricket, generally whole day games, began in 1950. The membership soon increased enough to enable a travelling side, aptly called The Strollers, to be fielded. It was lucky for the Club that Mr John Barker returned from his prisoner of war camp at the beginning of this development, as for the next twenty years he was the inspiration and driving force behind almost all the progress made at Lucas Lane.

In 1950 Mr F R Shillitoe, the Club Treasurer, died and this fact is mentioned because by then he and his father before him had filled the offices of Treasurer or Secretary continuously for some eighty years, surely a record of service unequalled by any other Club in the country.

With such facilities the social side of the Club became an important part of its activities, a development which encouraged an increase in the numbers of non-playing members. The Annual Dinner became a 'must' for most Club members and attracted such well known cricketers as Stuart Surridge, Frank Tyson, Douglas Insole, Ian Bedford, Peter Parfitt and John Clarke to reply to the toast to 'our guests'.

Additional gifts of land by Messrs Moss increased the size of the ground and though it was found impossible, at the time, to establish a second cricket table, there was a large playing area suitable for other games. The members of the Blueharts Hockey Club soon realised that, with sufficient space to establish four hockey pitches, the ground was ideal for use as their base and arrangements were made for them to use the ground during the winter months. From the early days the Clubs have worked closely together and are now reaping the benefits of shared expenses and ground equipment. But success demanded even better facilities and with Mr John Barker playing the leading role, plans went ahead with an extensive development which improved and modernised the pavilion and added an additional hockey pitch, equipment shed and car park. This was completed in 1965, just in time to allow the Club to do justice to its Centenary celebrations the following year. This was suitably commemorated, the highlight being the presence of Peter May and Jim Laker in a team which played in a special Centenary game on the ground.

During the 1970s and '80s the Club continued to develop. Joining the Hertfordshire League it probably has not yet done itself justice with coming second in 1976, its best achievement.

The completion of the construction of a second pitch in 1988, together with the formation of a ladies playing section, presents the Club with a great opportunity to expand its activities, particularly in terms of encouraging young cricketers.

The ground has for many years been the venue for Minor Counties and Gillette Cup (now National Westminster) games, including the wonderful occasion when Hertfordshire beat Essex. The Club has also concentrated on the hosting of benefit games to entertain the townspeople and improve its financial position. These are splendid events with the likes of Hadlee, Boycott, Gower, Lamb, Emburey, Fowler, Pringle and Ellison entertaining hundreds in front of as many as fourteen marquees on the banks.

Footnote

In 1994 the New Zealand team opened their tour with a match against Hitchin at Lucas Lane. Sadly, late in 1994 Frank Tromans died in his 80s. He had been associated with the Club for sixty years as player, Secretary and Vice President. As a French Master and cricket enthusiast at Hitchin Boys' School many a talented cricketing lad 'found' his way to Hitchin C C.

BUTTS CLOSE

'Butts Close, ten acres in extent, provides another delightful and restful public open space near the centre of the town'
Hitchin Official Guide 1921/2

Butts Close is the oldest open space in the town. By the end of the fourteenth century it was being used for games and was also where archery was practised – hence its name butts being the proper name for targets. Hitchin's historian, Reginald Hine, claimed that a company of archers were sent from Hitchin fought at Agincourt in 1415.

The Manor of Hitchin Portman and Foreign Extract from the Court Rolls:-
'That the occupier of every ancient Messuage or Cottage within the Township of Hitchin has a Right of Common for such Cattle, and at such time as are hereinafter specified upon the Greens Common and Lammas Meadows...
That any person having Right of Common may turn on the Green Common and Lammas Meadow Two Cows, One Bullock or Cow Calf under the age of two years...
That Butts Close is the sole Cow Common from the 6th day of April, being Old Lady Day, to the 12th day of May, also inclusive, and after that time is used for collecting in the morning the herd going to the other Common...'
Extract from 1899 'Handbook to Hitchin & the Neighbourhood'

These grazing areas live on in the names of The Meads, Lammas Mead and Bury Mead Road. The late Reverend Richard Lewis, the brother of Miss Violet Lewis, the last pharmacist at Perks & Llewellyn Chemists shop and Lavender Distillers in the High Street, recalled that between the wars the cow belonging to a landlord of the Rose and Crown in the Market Place could always find its own way from the fields to the public house.

Anthony Foster in his book 'Market Town' recorded that in 1730 smallpox claimed the lives of one hundred and fifty eight people. Conditions proved so bad that the market was temporarily transferred to the more airy Butts Close. He also noted that in the early years of the nineteenth century pupils from the Free School in Tilehouse Street were obliged to play football and cricket on Butts Close when they lost the use of their playground in Paynes Park.

Mr Matthews now living at Baldock and in his 80's recalls:-
'...Butts Close had two or three fairs each year plus the odd circus, ninety-nine times out of a hundred it used to rain......They always had them laid out on the lowest part...by the second night you were wallowing in mud.....'. Some things never change!

The avenue of pink flowered Horse Chestnuts was planted to coommemorate the coronation of King George VI and Queen Elizabeth, now the Queen Mother, which took place in 1937. The Lime trees around the Bedford Road edge of Butts Close were planted at the same time.

Derek Wheeler recalls. . . .
In the 1940s and early 1950s many of the trees which line the diagonal path had curious circular wooden seats around them which proved a delight to small children. In their imagination they could dream that they were back on the fairground roundabouts which rested close to the same spot two or three times a year. The fairground transport used to prove as interesting as the rides themselves for one could see ancient buses cannibalised to take throbbing generators, equipment, or more often than not, with curtained windows suggesting living accommodation. Here one could see exciting showmen's road locomotives made by Foster or Burrell, rocking gently, smelling sweetly, exuding majesty and power.

Above left and right: Carling and Hales' postcard of the tank 'Fearless': a common sight during a Sunday walk.
Left: C. Waldock postcard showing a rural-looking Butts Close in the 1920s.
Below: Photograph taken around 1890. A main attraction was surely the early steam-powered roundabout, probably sporting gaily painted 'gallopers'.

Above: Buffalo Bill and his Indians created a minor sensation by erecting their teepees on Butts Close. Placards outside the former 'Plough' in Bridge Street announce the arrival of the Wild West Show on June 23rd 1904. A great spectacle as 800 people and 500 horses took part! 'The equestrian sensation of modern times!'
Below: Looking north up Bedford Road in 1913, before the trees were planted on Butts Close.

No cows grazed here then but elephants, camels, horses and zebras could be seen irregularly as circuses came and went. In the immediate years following the 1951 Festival of Britain, once a year the Hitchin Show was laid out on the same site and also took over the fenced lawn upon which the new swimming pool now stands. A vast oval of green would be fenced off with chestnut palings and all the local organisations would have access to marquees where they could advertise themselves. The air in the canvas wonderland would be perfumed by the scent of the stock-in-trade of Harkness & Co, F A Wheeler & Son, The Horticultural Society, the Chrysanthemum Society, the Allotment Holders' Association, the Beekeepers with their glass sided hive, the cakemakers of the Townswomen's Guild and the embroiderers and spinners. Colour and fragance mingled with the barking of dogs, mewing of cats and the singing of a thousand canaries. At eleven in the morning everyone made a hasty exit from tents as the judges took over and the public returned at lunch-time to see the rosettes, the diplomas and the cups.

Outside, the children would amuse themselves with pony rides, miniature train rides given by the Hitchin Model Engineering Club, 'mini dipper' rides erected by RAF Henlow apprentices or watch fancy dress parades, folk and morris dancing. They might have seen the Festival Queen, Isobel Harkness presenting prizes, or the 1851 replica locomotive which had been constructed over a farm tractor for the Pageant celebrations. It was the event of the year.

Perhaps its successor was the annual carnival which followed on in the early 1960s, organised by a group of young people who called themselves the 'Local Yokels'. The carnival prize-giving ceremony has taken place each July since then on the high ground at the top of Butts Close.

Butts Close was separated from Elmside Walk until the early 1950s by a patch of allotments alongside the watercourse which was later transformed into the somewhat euphemistically styled 'ornamental pond' which in recent years has become a graveyard

Above: Drawing by Robert Walmsley (1922) showing Hitchin Grammer School's 'Swimsports' at the Queen Street Baths.

for shopping trolleys. This watercourse goes subterranean across the Boys' School field, into the Plantation and under Bancroft to join the Hiz to the rear of Bancroft car park. In the nineteenth century what is now the North Court at the Boys' School was a lake, presumably fed by this spring, which derives its water from the Gaping Hills. When the school field's level was raised in the mid-1950s the excavators found evidence of the nineteenth century mole draining, earthenware pipes of the same period and earlier bone drainage 'pipes'.

HITCHIN TOWN FOOTBALL CLUB

Excerpt from the Hitchin Town Football Club Supporters Club Annual 1957/58

Hitchin Town F C was founded back in 1865, twenty-one years before the Herts County F A was formed. Together with such famous old clubs as Queen's Park (Glasgow), Barnes Civil Service, Maidenhead, Clapham Rovers, Marlow and so on, Hitchin Town are proud to have been subscribers to the original F A Cup.

In July 1871 the F A resolved: 'That it is desirable that a challenge cup should be established in connection with the Association, for which all clubs should be invited to compete'. This was carried into effect, and the £25.00 necessary for the purchase of the Football Association Challenge Cup was subscribed by the clubs. Fifteen clubs, including Queen's Park (Glasgow), entered, and so did Hitchin Town.

After several seasons as an amateur club Hitchin decided to turn professional. In 1901 they became members of the newly-formed South-Eastern League, competing with clubs such as Luton Town, West Ham, Clapton Orient, Queen's Park Rangers, Millwall and Spurs. We find among the club's prominent members such stalwarts as W Hill, F A Wright, W Tindall-Lucas, F Shillitoe, T Ransom and A Amos who, incidentally, gained international honours.

In 1895 the Herts County Senior Cup first came to Hitchin, to be followed again in 1896, 1898, 1900 and 1903. Following a distrastrous start in 1903 they recovered splendidly to finish sixth place in the League, which had been strengthened by the inclusion of Watford, Brighton and Hove and a little- known side called Woolwich Arsenal. If the rise of the club was gradual its decline was swift. The Town could not support a professional or semi-professional team so shortly before World War One the club went out of existence and was not reformed until May 1928.

During the years between, Hitchin Blue Cross F C kept the flag flying, to be disbanded when the Town Club came into being again.

They were elected to the Spartan League in June 1928. Great strides were made. In the 1931-32 season they won the A F A Senior Cup, beating Derby Amateurs 6-0 in a replay, after a two all draw. Incidentally both games were played at Dulwich Hamlet's ground.

The club was at its strongest in 1939 when they gained admission to the Athenian League. To celebrate they won their first two league matches each with the extraordinary score of 7-1. On both occasions Southall F C were the unlucky victims. Sandwiched between these two victories was the 7-0 defeat of Letchworth in the Herts Charity Cup. Unfortunately the outbreak of World War Two stopped what promised to be a most successful season. During the war years Hitchin met with considerable success in the Herts-Middlesex League and in 1941 they won the championship.

After the war they returned to the Athenian League. The amateur soccer world was startled by their entry into the first round of the F A Cup (proper) and the quarter-finals of the Amateur Cup. Back in fighting trim again they became runners-up in the Athenian League with the best goal average.

Many famous players have worn the yellow jersey of the Town. There were goalkeeper Cecil Cannon who made more than fifty appearances for Herts County; Willie Westwood left-half and captain with over four hundred first team appearances; Eddie Armitage who scored eighty four goals (a club record) in season 1931-32; Les Clarke inside left, more than four hundred games and Claude Brown inside right, present trainer of the First Team.

The Town has always been famous for left wingers. Among them was Reggie Smith, who gained full international honours after signing as a professional for Millwall and was probably their most famous player. At present he is manager of Falkirk.

REDHILL ROAD

Almost certainly named after land called Red Hill Shott, Redhill Road was developed in the 1920's. Running west from the Bedford Road to its junction with Oughtonhead Lane, busy Redhill Road bears little resemblance to the 'beautiful lane which ran to Oughton Head' remembered by Hitchin people earlier in the century. At the beginning of the lane once stood the Victorian Nutleigh Grove House, (now the site of the Angel's Reply Public House). During the First World War this had served as a Battalion Headquarters for the Royal Engineers. Falling into disrepair it was demolished in the early 1960s. Its name lives on in Nutleigh Grove. Robert Walmsley remembers the lane ' ...along which girls who liked to entertain the military walked in their knee-high laced boots with bows at the top'.

Housing was urgently needed for the families in the Queen Street area. By 1930 the core of the new estate was in place, The Crescent being flanked by Westmill Road and the lower part of Mattocke Road. Housing needs continued to expand as families were moved from unsatisfactory cottages nearer the town centre and Hitchin itself grew in size. Much of the land had been owned by the Moss and Maidment families. The Urban District Council was progressive for its time and the new houses were spacious. Early examples were designed by Mr A T Blood, the Council Surveyor. Bathrooms were tucked into a space next to the kitchen and a wooden board could be lowered over the bath to provide an extra working surface!

Expansion continued well into the 1960's and the new Primary School, Oughtonhead, opened in 1965. Private housing was built during the early 1970's while many previous Local Authority tenants have since exercised their right to buy. Road names reflect respect for worthy Hitchin citizens of the past. Moss Way is connected with the Moss family of grocers, who owned land in the immediate area. Other associations include John Mattocke (Mattocke Road) founder of Hitchin's Free School (now the Hitchin Boys' and Hitchin Girls' Schools), Reginald Hine (Hine Way) Hitchin's historian, Mrs Swinburne (Swinburne Avenue) the first woman chairman of the HUDC in the 1960's and Mr J T Barker (John Barker Place) of the timber firm, who was Chairman of the Housing Committee in the 1950's and 1960's.

The Westmill estate lies adjacent to an area of great natural beauty and interest, long treasured by natives of the town. Close by are the springs which are the source of the River Oughton. At 1¾ miles in length it is possibly one of the shortest rivers in the country. It flows to Westmill Farm, on to Burford Way and under the Bedford Road to Ickleford where it joins the Hiz. Westmill Farm, now a private house, dates from the seventeenth century and was originally a water mill. Local tradition recalls the ghost of a girl who drowned herself after being jilted. Until late last century Oughtonhead Common was a 'Cow Common' on which certain town dwellers had a right of grazing. Every day between mid May and mid February cattle would be driven to the Common and allowed to stay until dusk. Such use, going back many centuries, had helped establish a huge variety of wild flowers and grasses. They in their turn attracted plentiful wildlife.

With the decline of grazing on the Common, (it ceased altogether about 1914) the carefully maintained grasslands slowly became overgrown. The demand for water has caused a dramatic fall in the water table over recent years resulting in the loss of wet grassland and marsh. Fortunately the decline of this area has come to the attention of the District Council and a proper management programme is now in operation. It may not be possible to recapture the past, but recently visitors must surely be encouraged by improvements.

Above: Nutleigh Grove House in 1949.
Right and below: Bedford Road in 1995, compared with a rare view of the same spot early in the century. On the right is Bearton lodge built in the 1820s.

For Teas and Refreshments try the

WALNUT TREE CAFÉ

REDHILL ROAD, HITCHIN

2 minutes from Town Football Field
50 yards off Main Bedford Road

Special attention to Cyclists and Motor Drivers (Cycles stored)

Parties catered for at moderate charges

Sweets and Cigarettes

Open on Sundays, 3 to 6 p.m. (Teas only)

Agent for Nott's famous Cakes and Pastries

Agent for "Country Side" Circulating Library

PROPRIETRESS, MRS. N. G. ROE

Above: Advertisement including photograph by T.B. Latchmore and Son appears in the 1931 Official Guide.
Above right: Front garden of Redhill Cottage. Four houses now stand on this site, the junction of Redhill Road and Oughtonhead lane.
Right: Peter Skipper, of Redhill Cottage. Mattocke Road can be seen in the background. Oughtenhead School and housing now occupy this field (1950s).
Below: Redhill Road in 1954.

BEARTON ROAD

Bearton (Old English 'bere-tun' or possibly 'burhtum') denotes a farm belonging to a burgh or fortified town. We know that Hitchin was a burgh by the twelfth century, though, of course, it may not have been fortified, and as a farm Bearton must have been important to it. On the 1818 Tithe map of Hitchin Bearton Homestead has six buildings. It was still a hamlet in the mid-nineteenth century being approached from Hitchin by a cartway, but by the 1900's it was absorbed into the town. There is a Bearton Farm on Hitchin's Ordnance Survey map of 1881.

It is worth remarking that one modern street plan depicts Bearton Avenue as traversing Lancaster Road and Lancaster Avenue and leading into Bearton Road. This did not come about, however, as modern day Bearton Avenue begins on Fishponds Road and ends as it meets Lancaster Road and Lancaster Avenue. A salutary lesson to us all in the use of maps as sources for local history.

By the last years of the nineteenth century the former cart-track to the hamlet of Bearton (off Bedford Road) was undergoing energetic development. Land became available field by field and was sold off as building plots. Local builders then erected houses in small terraces, or pairs, development starting at the York Road end.

A typical transaction recalls the sale of two plots of land in 1898 by 'Francis Frederic Lovell of Hincheslea, Brockenhurst, in the County of Southampton to Henry Cannon, confectioner of 92 Bancroft for one hundred pounds. The Indenture was witnessed by James Wakeford 'Butler to Mr Lovell'. Henry Cannon soon sold the land on at a profit and two houses were built by 1902, one being kept by the owner and one being sold. Restrictions on the use of the land decreed that 'no Inn, Tavern, Public House or Beershop' should appear on the site.

One of these plots is now number 18 Bearton Road. Interestingly, a faded postcard of the street, circa 1920, has the inscription 'photo by Mack's Studios, 18 Bearton Road, Hitchin' on the reverse. Mack's work also included photography for 'Phillips of Hitchin, Antiquarians, of the Manor House in Bancroft' (as cited in the Hitchin Household Almanack for 1915).

Suburbia had not entirely taken over. In his book 'Around 1919' Robert Walmsley remembers:-

'Along the Bedford Road was Brick Hills, called also Brick Kiln, lying at the junction with Bearton Road in that general area which had been called Bearton Green when I was young. Here was the deep flooded clay-pit which had supported a brick-yard and this was quite wild and unfenced and it provided children with an exciting play space but it was really dangerous, for it had steep sides and although there were a number of flat spots from which men and boys fished for roach, approach was difficult'.

Mrs Preston (née Sharp) also has childhood memories of the pond '....said to be the deepest for miles around, dangerous and not properly fenced'. She recalls seeing a man being pulled out '...a betting man who owed money'. The pond attracted its share of wildlife '...the road was nothing but frogs, you couldn't hardly walk for them. My mum was terrified'. More early recollections include the frozen surface in winter and skating '...not proper skating, sliding about'.

Mrs Preston's father, Mr Sharp, a General Foreman for Foster's, built numbers 105 and 106 for himself and his sister in 1928. Buying the plots he employed Foster's bricklayers, carpenters and plumbers to carry out the work during a slack time for the building firm, thus providing much needed work. Mrs Preston recalls that electricity did not arrive until

1930. Development continued steadily, the Hitchin Directory of 1926 listing one hundred and twenty two houses. Many residents chose house names, 'Riponia', 'The Rosary', 'St Helena', 'Kippington', and 'Seagary Villa' amongst others, giving an aura of settled suburban respectability to a road that had only been in existence for a quarter of a century.

Above: First World War postcard by H.G. Moulden, of Bearton Lodge in use as a Guard House for the Royal Engineers Signal Depot Camp.
Left and below: Royal Engineers at leisure and on parade.

OLD HALE WAY

Mr Studman recalls:

Bury Fields. . . . 'and there was a large field, we used to graze the cattle there, and it was big enough to have flying displays . . . one of those 'Flying Circuses' came there on one occasion, giving flights etcetera. . . flights to the public. . .

The old aircraft used to have a ski in front of them so they didn't bury the propeller into the ground when they landed. . . It must have been very early 1930s. . . .

Vickers Virginias at Henlow, canvas covers with the gunners all exposed, they used to come in low over Ickleford Road and came up over the old Blake's Theatre. . . quite thrilling really'.

Mrs Preston (née Sharp) remembers in the late 1920s:

'We used to pick armfuls of andelions in the fields by Wallace's cows. Mum made andelion wine, it tasted better than any whisky, so father said!'

Right: Vickers Virginia.
Below: Outside Mrs Maude Callington's house in the 1920s (No. 73). Looking towards Ickleford, on the left, is the site of Strathmore School. Strathmore Avenue is on the right (by the telegraph pole).

Above: Mrs Prebble's bungalow (No. 52) in 1945. Her daughter has happy memories of bluebell picking in the meads, and the nearby dell.
Left: range (pattern 'G') in situ at 101, since the house was built in the early 1930s.
Below: The splendid Aurora Bungalow Range, the instructions provide for cooking, hot water and an open fire.

The "AURORA" Bungalow Range.

Pattern "G."

WORKING INSTRUCTIONS.

CLEANING INSTRUCTIONS

POINTS TO REMEMBER

HITCHIN RUGBY CLUB

As remembered by BAJ Chapman

Founded in 1954, the club started from a meeting held at the Red Hart Hotel.

Maurice Dolden had just been appointed Headmaster at the Boys' Grammar School and the meeting was in response to his appeal in the Herts Pictorial that it would be appropriate to form a Club at a time when Rugby Football was being introduced to the school.

Sufficient members were present for a Committee to be formed and shortly after the Council made a pitch available at King George V playing fields. It was proposed that the team would change at the neighbouring Territorial Army Hut.

The choice of the Club's colours and badge rests, almost certainly, with the late George Evans (Librarian to North Herts and Curator of the Museum) who, in his own words, had 'the undeserved status of the Club's aesthetic arbiter'. At the time he had a passion for maroon as a livery colour (all the mobile libraries at the time were maroon) and felt the regimental uniformity of maroon shirts with white collars, white shorts and maroon socks would strike fear into the hearts of opponents.

The hedgehog, the Club's emblem, was chosen as being both apposite and unique. The term 'Hertfordshire Hedgehog', used to describe the inhabitants of North Hertfordshire, goes back a long way. In the country dialect a 'hedgehog' was a stout club and the men of North Hertfordshire were noted for their clannish and prickly behaviour. The hedgehog seemed very appropriate as the badge of Hitchin Rugby Club.

The Club was developed to running a second team in 1955 and on 8 September 1962 opened its own clubhouse. However, following the great effort that this required, relaxation set in and by 1966 the Club was in a poor state. At the conclusion of the 1966/67 season the Club bar had taken a total of £169.00 and the players' shirts from the last game in April were still on the changing room floor at the AGM in June. The late sixties were difficult years but gradually renewed effort turned the scales and was the start of twenty-five years progress to the present day.

With a strengthening in numbers, additional pitches were sought and a series of extensions made to the clubhouse. The Club now has three of the best rugby pitches in Hertfordshire.

The increase in the playing membership by 1973 had been the outcome of the Club's policy to seek to do everything as well as it possibly could. Even the introduction of cricket for members in 1968, and still an active part of the Club year, helped to advertise the club in the neighbourhood. This was also the period when Bob Airey, a coach from New Zealand, joined the Club. He, more than anybody, changed the playing attitude of the Club and brought it of age.

Hitchin is a Club that involves a large part of its membership in administering its affairs. This is very necessary because it has grown to having five Senior Sides, a Colts XV, a Ladies playing section and an ever-increasing Mini/Junior Section. This growth has given rise to more ambitious activity, externally in County rugby affairs where it has achieved an impressive reputation for hosting County Championship Games and County Tournaments, and internally where, for example, rugby tours such as that to Nuits St Georges (Hitchin's twin town) in 1980 and the USA in 1990 have grown to the extent that at Easter 1995 the men's team went to Budapest, the ladies to Amsterdam and one hundred and thirty-five Mini/Juniors, with parents, went to Dublin.

The outstanding event in the Club's history is undoubtedly the privilege of appearing at Twickenham on Saturday 3 April 1993 to

Above: The Club's First XV 1954/55.

contest the Provincial Cup Final against Fleetwood RFC from Lancashire. At the outset of the Competition five hundred and twelve of the sixteen hundred Junior Rugby Clubs in England were eligible to compete. To win through to the Final, to be party to the grand occasion, to play on the playing field that is the centre of world rugby, to share the experience with thousands of supporters from the town and, despite a defeat (7-13), it was a day of great rejoicing. The practical support the club received from the town, from its businesses and from the Council, resulted in a substantial extension being built to the Clubhouse, which is a permanent reminder to all who were party to the event.

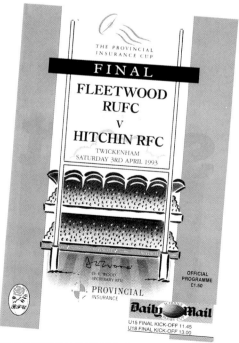

STRATHMORE AVENUE

As remembered by Mrs Masters:
'To begin with, before the houses were built on what is now known as Strathmore Avenue, there were fields. These contained cows and the fields belonged to Wallace's. The fields were spread out all over this area. Where the end of Whitehurst Avenue is now, was a big bank.

The houses in Strathmore Avenue were built around 1939. The houses were built going up the Avenue. The man who built the houses was called Mr Fred Pettengell. At the time he had built four on this side and these were numbered from 53-59. He also built ten on the other side which were numbered from 58-78. This is when the war broke out and Mr Pettengell was halfway through building numbers 61 and 63 Strathmore Avenue when he died.

The colour of the street lamps seemed different, more of an orange colour, this later changed. The road was concrete, then there were the grass verges and then the cinder pathway. At this time there was electricity and gas in Strathmore Avenue.

The tree which is situated outside number 59 Strathmore Avenue is not the original. One day, when there was a lot of rain, the trunk did not look stable. So this was taken down and a new tree was put up. This tree is the one that is there today. This took seven men to come and pull the tree up – three men to dig it up – and four men to watch!

The parade of shops that are in Strathmore Avenue were there in 1939. They were built by Willmotts. The flats which are now opposite were originally going to be shops. This was when the war came and they became flats.

When the war finished there was a party put on in the street, tables were put out and a big party was had for the children.

The houses behind the odd numbered side of Strathmore Avenue were originally there, this was Wilton Road. Then you could see clearly all around as there were not many trees in this area'.

Far right: Advertisement from Official Handbook of the District Council for Hitchin, 1912.
Right and below: Mrs Masters with Miss Hunt spring-cleaning their manhole cover for the Historical Society photographer. Fred Pettengell built many of the houses in Strathmore Avenue.

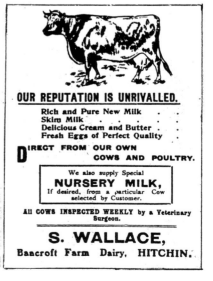

OUR REPUTATION IS UNRIVALLED.

Rich and Pure New Milk . .
Skim Milk . . . . . .
Delicious Cream and Butter . .
Fresh Eggs of Perfect Quality .

DIRECT FROM OUR OWN
        COWS AND POULTRY.

We also supply Special
NURSERY MILK,
If desired, from a particular Cow
selected by Customer.

All COWS INSPECTED WEEKLY by a Veterinary
Surgeon.

S. WALLACE,
Bancroft Farm Dairy, HITCHIN.

LANCASTER ROAD

In the autumn of 1897 the schedule of the Deed of Conveyance for a plot of land in Lancaster Road stipulates that ". . . no house shall be built thereon at a less cost than one-hundred-and-fifty pounds including the cost of suitable offices (lavatory and washing facilities) and outbuildings". The house that was built on the site - 'Aldersyde' - is one of the grandest in the street and like several other houses in Lancaster Road, still has its bootscraper by the gate.

Shortly after the building of York Road, terraces of houses were completed along Lancaster Road. In 1907 the Hertfordshire Express announced the development of the Fishponds Estate, when thirty-two acres of land became available for building. This included part of Fishponds Road and the continuation of Lancaster Road into Lancaster Avenue. By 1915 the Hitchin Household Almanack shows twenty-eight houses completed in the Avenue, named but as yet un-numbered. Lancaster Road ran from numbers one to seventy-four.

Right: Early business advertisement.
Below: Turn-of-the-century postcard. Notice the grocer's shop still trading on the same site today.

Shorthand & Typewriting

TAUGHT IN HITCHIN AND STEVENAGE.

Terms moderate.   First Class Tuition.   Class or Private Lessons.
SERMONS and MSS. of all descriptions Typewritten.
Estimates, &c., taken from Dictation.

EWART G. CULPIN, 3 LANCASTER ROAD, HITCHIN.

LANCASTER RD HITCHIN

Above: Lancaster Road, 1910, at end nearest York Road.
Some attractive architectural details are to be found in this road.
Centre and lower left: Porch arch with decorative keystone showing detail of the 'Green Man' type face.

Right: Detail from arch over entrance to the Digrado Hotel. The intials 'JFP' also occur on properties in York Road. Who was he?

YORK ROAD

The fourteenth and fifteenth century Dukes of York had involvement with Hitchin Manor and they are in part commemorated by York Road, as it is in connection with the Wars of the Roses (1455 - 85) that York Road and the adjacent Lancaster Road are so named.

Built on arable land, York Road must have been constructed mostly between 1886 and 1900. It does not appear on an 1886 map of Hitchin compiled by George Beaver. Some of the houses in this road were built in 1897 and one 1896 Deed of Conveyance tells us that the plot of land is '...situate with a frontage to a new road running from Dukes Lane to the Ickleford Road'.

York Road is interesting in that the style of building reflects a prosperity in late Victorian Hitchin. Each house has its carefully chamfered window lintel, its Tudor rose decoration and its elaborate ridge tiles and finials. The houses are built for the perambulator and bicycle age, for there is no rear access for ponies (or motor cars) in most cases. The front gardens are just big enough to house enough plants to brighten the bay windows and the rear gardens are long enough to support vegetables and maybe afford sufficient light for a greenhouse or two. No commercial premises were allowed to 'lower the tone' of this road, indeed, early planning restrictions stipulated that '...no Inn, Tavern... may be built...'. The children of the Victorian era had a fair way to travel to school, The Gainsford St Saviour's school in Radcliffe Road being somewhat nearer than the British or St Mary's Schools in the town centre. This was to change when the Wilshere Dacre School was erected on arable land in 1928 and the York Road Nursery was opened at the beginning of World War Two. This temporary building, which is still with us, was originally conceived as a creche for the children of women munitions workers, since most local engineering works were turned over to round-the-clock production. Its air raid shelter still stands; interestingly enough it is now used as the staff room.

St Luke's Home of Rest

This institution was founded at a house in York Road in September 1897 by Miss Thackthwaite, where accommodation was provided for seven inmates, the object being to provide a home for aged women who could contribute a portion towards the cost of living. In 1898 larger and more commodius premises were taken in Walsworth Road and the usefulness of the institution was extended. Convalescent patients were admitted for long or short periods and ladies could have private apartments. Residents in Hitchin, as dormitory inmates, were charged seven shillings a week. Miss Thackthwaite was Head of the Home, assisted by an efficient staff. There are a few voluntary subscribers and more would be acceptable.

Hitchin Household Almanack Directory 1899

Foster's – The Builders

The one employer in the road has long since gone; Foster's the builders. The late Tony Foster, historian, has written about the family firm. A good many schools in the county owe their premises to this firm and Royal Air Force stations and government building contracts kept Foster's busy throughout the immediate post war years.

The earliest Fosters in the town were wheelwrights operating certainly in the 1780's. By 1880 William Foster and his three sons had a successful family business in carpentry on Park Street. During the 1920's their enterprise was taken over by A V Duller. This family is thought by Pat Gadd, one of our contemporary historians, to have been close relatives of Matthew and F O Foster.

Advertisements from the Handbook to Hitchin and its Neighbourhood (1897) *demonstrating the wide variety of skills held by the firm.*

Matthew Foster had premises in Bancroft, where, in 1891, there was a disastrous fire graphically reported in the diary of the Hitchin Fire Brigade, then under the captaincy of Isaac Chalkley. Foster had time to remove his family and to secure his safe and books but the whole of his stock and premises were soon engulfed in flames which spread to Messrs Ellis & Everard, which adjoined Foster's yard. Foster's horse died in the fire and one man in a loft was injured when he fell. A large quantity of workmen's tools were lost, which were not insured so a collection was made.

The firm is probably best known for the building of the new Town Hall. Built in red brick stone in 1901 the whole cost, including the land, was £7,300. The design was drawn up by architect Geoffrey Lucas, a relative of the Quaker brewing family, and E V Lucas.

Matthew Foster also built the new Post Office in Brand Street in 1904. Before this the Post Office had been in West Alley or Post Office Alley and then in the Market Place.

Probably the most illustrous visitor to the road was Bob Hope, the famous American film star and comedian, who regularly used to visit relatives in the area. On one occasion he paid a brief visit to York Road School, much to the delight of children and parents.

A conversation with Miss Mollie Hancock, now resident at The Old Rectory Retirement Home, Graveley.

'My parents came to live at Number 5 York Road in 1907 or '08. At that time York Road was rather like the lower end of The Avenue and my parents were not sure which to choose. I was born in 1910 at Number 5 which is a creeper-covered house.

In the days when I was a child all the passing traffic through our road was horse-drawn and all goods were delivered by this means. The butcher called every day and we had Cooper's. There were two brothers named Cooper and they had shops in Tilehouse Street and Bancroft. The shop in Tilehouse Street had fine tiling on either side and can still be seen today, it came to belong to Brookers. There were two other butchers, Allingham's and Ansell's.

Each day cows from Wallace's Farm (the field can be seen in the background of the photograph) made four trips to and fro through York Road for milking. You might be able to count up to ninety-nine cows but there was never a hundred. The other entrance to the field was in Bancroft where Wallace's had their Dairy.

In those days there were no buildings from York Road to the Railway Bank and with aviation in its infancy this huge flat area of land was used to land bi-planes which caused much excitement to all us children - the novelty was a great thrill, which we would all rush to see.

In the middle of the area known as The Meads was a lovely pond where I went with friends and spent many happy hours fishing for newts and tadpoles.

I lived in York Road until 1940, by this time my father had died and my mother and I went to live in Grays Lane.'

Miss Hancock is a founder member of the Hitchin Art Club and is still an active member of the Club which celebrated its Fiftieth Anniversary in 1993. She is also a member of The Thursday Club.

Above and inset: Postcard dated 1909 drawing attention to the delights of the Palace Theatre. Left: Photograph dated 1922 showing the procession of Wallace's cows through the street. The little girl on the left is Joan Newbury who grew up to run a dancing school.

BUNYAN ROAD

Bunyan Road, like many others, is named after someone with local connections. The tinker of Elstow, John Bunyan (1628 - 88), preached in this area, especially in the original Tilehouse Street Chapel and, of course, in the Dell which bears his name in Wain Wood. His 'Pilgrim's Progress' has local geographical features veiled in its narrative. Bunyan Road appears on the 1886 map of Hitchin but not on that of 1851.

The road has its Victorian origin in the infill ribbon development which linked the town centre to the railway station. Most of the houses date from the late Victorian period, some still have datestones visible. While Fishponds Road seems to have been developed to suit the professional classes, Bunyan Road furnished those of more modest income with a sturdy dwelling; terraced cottages being buttressed by 'villas'.

Until the 1960s the road used to have gas lighting. The Pirton baker, still delivering by pony cart until this date, used the green lamp posts to tether his pony. In the war years these same posts had dustbins chained to them so that domestic scraps could be saved for pig swill.

At the York Road end was a butchery run by a striking character called Joe Brinklow. He habitually wore brown leather gaiters and popular legend suggested he had been kicked at some time by a cow. He was a key horseman in the 1951 Hitchin Pageant, a thousand years of local history spectacularly staged in the lovely grounds of the Priory. The butchery and grocery business later continued under Eric Dyer and latterly Peter Foskett.

In the front parlour of number 37 there was a barber's shop and childhood memory could easily supplant Mr Swannell by Sweeney Todd! He had a gas light which glinted off his cut-throat razor and a very basic chair. This was of oak construction, almost vertical, with a rudimentary head rest. A plank would be placed across the arms if a wailing toddler was to be given a 'short back and sides' because Mr Swannell was very good at basic barbering. On Mondays, which was a quiet day, he could be seen, Chad-like, peering up and down the road over the curtain rail which half hid his trade secrets from the outside world, almost saying 'Wot! No trade?'

There was a band leader who gave pleasure to thousands in the frenzied air of wartime hops in the Town Hall. Wilson Hill, who led a band called 'The Aces', lived half-way down the road on the left at number 49. In his tiny front room, measuring no more than ten feet square, he had a settee and a grand piano on which he gave lessons.

Like many roads in this area, there were railway families who had settled here at the turn of the century. In the post-war period there was a railway pensioner, Mr Osborne, who proudly wore a gold watch and chain. He lived at number 19 and could remember open footplates on locomotives. At number 20 lived Mr Gray senior who had been responsible for construction work on the railways, in the same house lived 'Bowly' Blindell, another railway worker. Next door lived Mr Gray junior who was an engine driver. He pursued a hobby which is almost dead now. He had a 'Hobbies' treadle fret machine and his house and shed were a temple to this type of woodwork. Displayed in his front window was a magnificent wooden mainline model locomotive, and in the shed one could see fretwork soldiers painted in the colours of their respective regiments, acting out static battles of long ago.

Two residents of the road had seen a change in their lives which was typical of many families, the transition from country dweller to town dweller. Fred Weston and his wife Rose, resident from the 1930s to the late 1960s, had come from families whose roots were in domestic service. Fred had followed his father's profession as keeper on the Delmé-Radcliffe estate and had lived at Wellbury cottages along the Hexton Road. His wife's family had worked on the Rothschild estates in Buckinghamshire and the two met while she was visiting a children's nurse at Highdown House. When Fred joined the army in the First World War, the keeper's cottage had to be vacated and on return from the army the job had gone too. He had a change of employment working for a time as a chauffeur to a tea company executive in Chiltern Road, moving as the employer moved and settling back in Hitchin as employment became available, at Shelvoke & Drewry in Letchworth. Wartime

Below: A wonderful photograph of Bunyan Road with some of its young residents, taken at the turn of the century.
Left: The same view, taken in 1995. Note that the modern lamp-post occupies the same spot as its predecessor.

armaments manufacture at George King's in Walsworth Road saw him at an engineering bench and old age saw him working as a gardener at Victaulic. Like so many of their generation, rented accommodation was all that the 'Land fit for Heroes' had to offer and retirement at sixty- five was an impossibility.

The gas lamps have gone, the outside toilets and coal shed too. The houses have now gone into private ownership and a new prosperity has seen the Victorian façades being given a clean here, a colour wash there. The baker could no longer tether his pony, the motor car has reduced the width of the road to a bridle path, the tiny gardens cannot supply parking space for modern needs!

Right: Grandma Priscilla Gatward on the occasion of Priscilla Ayres christening in 1905. Grandma Gatward, a maternity nurse, lived in Bunyan Road.
Far right: Fred and Rose Weston in the garden of their home at Number 18.
Below right: A fine array of chimney pots!
Below: A selection from an early Broad & Co catalogue; right, an interesting cluster of pots of varying heights, materials and colours to be seen on the roof of a house in Bunyan Road.

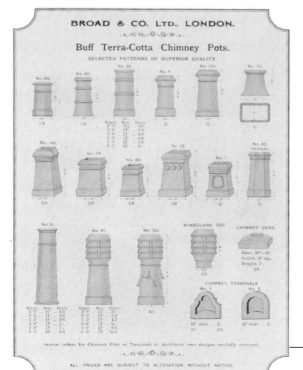

BROAD & CO. LTD., LONDON.

Buff Terra-Cotta Chimney Pots.

SELECTED PATTERNS OF SUPERIOR QUALITY

FISHPONDS ROAD

This road adjoins land once called Fishpond Closes or Little Fishpond Close and Great Fishpond Close. In one of these there was a pond formed from the Capswell Brook, now culverted (a culvert is a tunnel-drain for water crossing a road), which rises on Butts Close and joins the River Hiz somewhere behind the Skynners' Almshouses. The pond existed as an ornamental lake in the grounds of 'Woodside', Bancroft, now Hitchin Boys' School, until about 1929.

The 1898 Ordnance Survey map shows development in Fishponds Road to consist solely of a neat row of villas stretching down the north side of the road to the junction with Bunyan Road. By 1900 building had begun opposite.

Site of Wilshere Dacre School

Older residents in the 1940's could remember Butts Close and the Grammar School and Wilshere Dacre fields being used for grazing. Photographs show Wallace Brothers' cows being led down the road at milking time to enter the farmyard at the bottom of Fishponds Road. The entrance to this farm was still there in the 1950s, remaining as a track beside the bus garage which led past the old cowsheds, used at that time as storage by the telephone engineers, and emerging between the old Regal cinema and the Bancroft Dairy.

The Victoria pub used to be run by 'Bunt' Turner who had a corn chandlery business in its yard. Here chickens would strut lazily among the bags of corn while surrounding walls supported those indestructible enamel signs advertising 'Ovum' or 'Spratts' dog biscuits.

Mr Matthews of Baldock has memories from the 1920's of the field where Wilshere Dacre School (built 1928) now stands:-

'We often used to go up there and..... play football and such like....it was just an open field... . I remember going to one fair there because there was one of those people who used to dive from a terrifically high ladder into a small pond of water, all on fire. They used to light the fire on the water and he used to light himself up in a fire-proof suit and dive off there into the water. As soon as he hit the water the waves used to put the fire out and put his fire out as well. He used to do it twice a night! I think it was seven o'clock and nine o'clock - very daredevil - crowds used to gather there. The fair was free to go to in the open field'.

Jubilee House

In 1894 Alfred Ransom sold nine plots of land on the south side of Fishponds Road. Plots one and two, which had a total frontage of sixty-two feet eight inches, were sold to Mrs Margaret Sturrock Phillips for £180.

A house, Faith Lodge, was built for Mrs Phillips on this land in 1897. However, from a sketch which appeared in *'The Builder'* of 3 June 1899, the property seems to have been used as an Old Folks' Home.

In 1922 Mrs Phillips sold Faith Lodge to Hugh and Amyas Phillips of the Manor House, Hitchin for £735. A Deed of Exchange of Property was drawn in 1936 whereby Amyas Phillips gave Hugh Phillips various properties including '...that piece of land on the south side of Fishponds Road formerly known as Faith Lodge and now known as *Chavenage*.

Hugh Phillips sold the property in 1962 to KGT Investment Company Ltd, whose offices were at 20 Bancroft. Between 1962 and 1983 the house had several owners during which time its name changed to *Checkpoint*. In 1983 North Herts District Council purchased the property for £65,000 since which time it has been used as short-term accommodation for single people. The Council asked the pupils of nearby Wilshere Dacre School to find a new name for the house. They chose *'Jubilee House'* in honour of Queen Victoria's Diamond Jubilee in 1897, the year in which the house was built.

Left: Angel Crest from Jubilee House.
Above: Charming terracotta house tiles.
Right: Sketch of John Wilshere by Samuel Lucas.
Below and centre left: A peaceful Fishponds Road detailed on a 1915 postcard from Mack's studio, Bearton Road. Notice the bashful road sweeper hidden beneath his cart.
Centre right: The same view, 1995.

FISHPONDS ROAD

BANCROFT RECREATION GROUND

The gem in the once Hitchin Urban District Council (now NHDC) crown must surely be the Bancroft Recreation Ground. In the 1900's it was osier beds and nurseries, diagonally crossed by a path known as the ' Gas Path', since the old gas works were at Starlings Bridge. Purchased in 1924, 'the rec' flourished. Through the years, the HUDC, the North Herts Council and latterly Tyler's of Royston have kept this picturesque spot immaculate, a cornucopia of colour. In the 1950's woe betide a child who stepped over the ankle-high steel cable fences to retrieve a ball, ignoring all cast iron 'Keep Off' notices! The groundsmen were always on the scene to make sure their handiwork was maintained to a high standard.

Children started their playing days in 'the rec', pram-pushing mothers would let loose white sun-hatted toddlers to make their first eager steps across the velvet, daisy-free grass. Older children would play on the swings or sail boats on the pond which was regularly drained and cleaned. Older girls would tuck their dresses into their navy knickers and paddle or do handstands against the wooden walls of the shelter. Teenagers would book the tennis courts for a summery game; the middle-aged would play bowls on the Cumberland turf and the elderly would sit in the shade or take tea in the quaint pavilion. At weekends the bandstand would echo to the sound of Sousa or Sullivan. The Bancroft car park was then nurseries and orchard, with a small woodland walk along the bank of the Hiz. A rudimentary toilet existed backing onto the gasworks wall and a drinking fountain supplied cold summer sustenance near the shelter. From the 1960's onwards the council play scheme used to run putting activities and painting competitions in 'the rec'.

Postcard dated 1931 showing an immaculate expanse of pond, the early play equipment can be seen in the background.

Children in 1995 enjoying the new play equipment. The old swings and seesaw together with the paddling pool have all vanished. Below: Concentration on the Bancroft Bowling Green (Hitchin Official Guide 1962/3).

Less tranquil times saw the age of the vandal when the shelter suffered and the pool became unsafe for paddling, as more and more bottles broke on its concrete bottom. The pool went as the skateboard arrived; and national legislation dictated that the play areas should have safe surfaces for apparatus to rest on. The old pavilion is still there, enhanced and enlarged by the addition of the function hall. The groundsmen are much less officious now and the gates are not locked at dusk! This always seemed a pointless exercise since the iron railings had been removed in the wartime scrap drive and never replaced!

This is a magic eight and a half acre plot where our wise ancestors catered for the recreation of every age before leisure centres were ever dreamed of, before most people even had leisure! He who wrote the Official Guide for 1931 could come back and reflect on his words today:-

'If you are weary you can turn into our new Recreation Ground and sit at ease in its gardens and watch the city fathers at their bowls and the young men at their tennis'

ICKLEFORD ROAD

Clifford Offer, author of 'King Offa in Hitchin', (1992), tells us that 'Ickleford' means 'the ford of Icel'. Icel was the founding figure in Penda's seventh century Mercian dynasty, though family trees in this context were never 'gospel truth'. Although the road heads in the Ickleford direction, it has never been a main route to the village.

Building in Ickleford Road followed the pattern of development in the adjacent Bunyan Road, and together with the houses at the lower end of Fishponds Road, they formed the core of the new residential streets on the north-west flank of Bancroft. Two cottages (numbers 65 and 66) on the eastern side of the road were built by 1862; deeds showing change of ownership indicate that their land stretched down to Water Lane. This pair appear on the 1886 map. By 1898 houses had appeared on the western side of the road. Plots of land had been sold for individual development. Numbers 35 and 36, for example, were built on land bought at auction at the Sun Hotel in August 1896. Mr Francis Lovell of Brockenhurst received £105.00 for Lot 3 from Henry Cox. Mr and Mrs Cox had two houses built on their plot, they occupied number 35 themselves, Henry until he died in 1937 and his widow, Elizabeth until 1957. Interestingly this house has had only three owners. Henry Cox's initials stand over the door. Henry Cox is remembered by his nephew, Mr John Long, as a dapper little man who was a strict Victorian disciplinarian and a churchwarden at St Mary's Church, who always insisted on Grace before meals. He was a Rate Collector which gave him insight into people's financial positions and he gave a lot of financial advice to both lenders and borrowers.

By 1898 building on the western side of the road was almost complete to the junction with Duke's Lane, twenty-seven houses in total. Beyond Duke's Lane, four pairs of larger semi-detached villas had appeared, on larger plots and set further back from the road. Building appears to have been completed by the outbreak of the First World War. The Victoria Public House, number 1 in the road, was first licensed in 1865 when it was known as The Cricketers.

Mr Studman remembers:–

'I was at Ickleford Road Post Office at that time. My father and aunt ran that between them....right on the corner near the Bancroft end.... at the back, directly behind our garden, there was a laundry, Mr and Mrs Frazer used to run it, they had very antiquated machinery, all made of wood - that was in the early 1930's .... I think it disappeared before the war. It used to be full of steam, dampness and wet. I think it was just the man and wife there. They had a long sort of garden place where they used to hang all the washing out. They lived in one of the cottages in Nightingale Road.'

Blake's Theatre

Ickleford Road is a mainly residential area, the exception being the old Blake's Theatre. Opening in March 1911 it was originally a 'Picturedrome' built by William (Bill) and Ernie Blake and was one of the first buildings to be erected as a permanent cinema. The first blockbuster to be screened there was the film of the 1911 Coronation celebrations in Hitchin made by the Blakes themselves.

The stage revolved and at the time was one of the best in the country outside London. It boasted its own orchestra under the direction of 'Teddy' Mayes, Hitchin's Bandmaster and a noted cornet player. On the same bill as the film shows the Picturedrome also staged variety acts and music hall turns including the great Marie Lloyd. On Saturday nights boxing contests were held and in the 1920's trapeze artists performed. Children were given sweets at the matinées and at Easter presented with an Easter egg.

In October 1913, the Hitchin Playhouse opened in the Market Place as a rival to Blake's but the Picturedrome continued to thrive. Improvements were made which included the addition of a gallery to the original single floor and a new tall front elevation. It was claimed that the 'New Picturedrome' was the most central, the best ventilated and, with ten exits, the safest cinema in town! In the 1920s the Playhouse was taken over by the Blake brothers and because it was more central and Hitchin was not big enough to support two theatres, the Picturedrome was eventually closed. The Blakes continued to own the property until 1935 when Bill died.

Blake's Theatre, as it had by now become known, came under the control of a Dovercourt company, but was never used as a cinema again. The licence it had held under the 1907 Cinematograph Act had expired and extensive alterations were required for its renewal under the 1935 Act. Instead, in 1938, for a short time, stage plays were performed. These consisted of travelling repertory companies with an Edgar Wallace thriller, a variety show and plays such as 'Uncle Tom's Cabin' and - a real must - 'Murder in the Red Barn', described by many who saw this as '...out of this world...'!

Mr Studman remembers that '....during the war it became a cookhouse for the Army, then after that it became a storehouse for food. .....at one time they had a circus there, they had to open the back entrance to get the elephants in. They had to borrow some barrels from a brewery to put under the stage to take the weight of the elephants...... the elephants

Right: Ickleford Road showing the original frontage of Blake Bros. Picturedrome.

Far right: Bay window surmounted by imposing castellations.
Below: Some door lintels tell a story! Initials of Henry Cox above the door of Number 35 proudly proclaim ownership of the house built around 1896. JBF over the door at Number 36 are believed to stand for John Bunting Franks who bought the house from Henry Cox in 1897 for £350. His widow sold it in 1918 to William Abbiss, well-known in Hitchin as a swimming instructor and at_hlete.

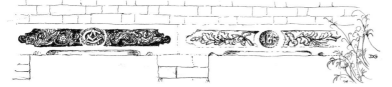

were stored somewhere, they used to bring them through the streets and make the one behind hang onto the tail of the one in front, the last one had a lantern hanging on his tail because it was dark when they were bringing them back at night'. Mr Matthews of Baldock says: 'It was a typical cinema of those days, very poor ventilation - you could smell that you'd been to the cinema for days afterwards - tobacco smells .... when they put the projector on you could see a pointed cone of smoke - blue smoke'!

Until 1963 it remained derelict. Blake's Theatre still stands today but is used as offices and a thriving gymnasium and fitness club. The Blakes are not forgotten. This spot has been known as 'Blake's Corner' since 1973 and the name appears on the Post Office next door to the former Picturedrome.

Above: 1916 view of Blake's Theatre showing its new front elevation.
Below left: The 1960's 'improvements' to the same building (photographed 1995).
Left: The circus comes to town! This elephant is about to quench its thirst at the fountain in Bedford Road.

WILLIAM ABBISS, THE GYMNASIUM, HITCHIN.

Member of the National Society of Physical Education.

By Examination, Theory and Practice.
Diploma for British and German Systems, also First Class Certificate for Swedish Educational Gymnastics.

Visits Schools and Classes in the Neighbourhood.
Private Classes arranged for Children or Adults.
Remedial and Corrective Work undertaken from qualified Medical Diagnosis.
Fourteen years' practical experience.

Private Address : **Icknield, Ickleford Road, HITCHIN.**

Above: Advertisement from 1915 Almanack and Directory. Incidentally, 'Icknield' refers to Number 36 (see previous page).

Hitchin's Other Cinemas

In addition to the Picturedrome, Hitchin possessed three other cinemas; the Playhouse in the Market Place, the Hermitage in Hermitage Road and the Regal in Bancroft.

The Playhouse opened in 1913 with seating for 750 in the stalls and balcony with a private box seating five on each side towards the back. The auditorium was lavishly decorated with an elaborate painting in the centre of the ceiling. It closed in 1937, supposedly for alterations, but never re-opened. The frontage was

absorbed until 1978 by Burtons the tailors. In 1985 the newsagents Lavells occupied the area which has since been taken over by Martin's and the town's main Post Office since it moved from Hermitage Road.

Strangely enough, it was the Post Office which occupied a site adjoining the Hermitage, which was in business from 1932 - 1963. It could seat 1386 and also boasted a full-size stage, orchestra pit and a dozen dressing rooms. It had an excellent position and the best arrangements in town. At one time the Hitchin Thespians put on their productions here.

The Regal opened in 1939 and had an ultra-modern frontage and seating for 1055 but it closed each summer for staff holidays. It shut as a cinema in 1977 but re-opened in 1980 after having been converted into a recording studio and concert hall but eventually folded. As a rare

Left: Playhouse Theatre in the market square.
Below: An august gathering for the Fourth Annual Review at the Playhouse on 19th November 1929. Left to Right: E J Anderson, Capt W G Wilcox, Admiral of the Fleet Earl Jellicoe, Lady Myrtle Jellicoe, Stanley Lee, Mr P H Devitt, Mr R Delmé-Radcliffe, Admiral Sir Lionel Halsey.

● North Hertfordshire's Acknowledged
Centre of Entertainment . . . .

THE

HERMITAGE
CINEMA

AND CAFÉ

H I T C H I N

●

PHONE 525

●

THE LUXURY CINEMA
WITH PERFECT SOUND

*Above left: The Hermitage in
the summer of 1932.
Left: The Regal in 1979.
Above: Advertisement from
1936/37 Hitchin Official
Guide.*

and good example of 1930's architecture in
Hitchin, applications were made to have
the building listed by the Department of
the Environment but to no avail and it was
eventually demolished to make way for
flats and a doctors' surgery now called
Regal Chambers.

GROVE ROAD

Grove Road was built as a residential street at the end of the Victorian era on land that had been a nursery. A small part of it still has this 'transitional' use and is a garden centre. The path that had gone through the area might have been called Sweetbriar Lane. Hearsay has it that the blacksmith at the Woolpack public house half-a-century ago remembered Grove Road as having this name.

Mrs Nellie Coxall (née Charles), born in 1901 remembers: '...Jimmy Knight, he built some houses in Grove Road and mother took one of these...we had my father and two brothers in the house...father was doing twelve hours a day, six in the morning until six at night, six at night until six in the morning'. (Mr Charles was a Railway Inspector.)

Mrs Ford has vivid memories of her childhood in Grove Road before the Second World War: '...Alderman's Dairy was in Grove Road where the dog parlour is now...there was a bridge over the river from Ransom's 'rec' with cows going into the dairy, I remember the cows being milked and in later years the ice cream they used to make and sell...the old stone floor and the steps going up to the house...Abbiss Nurseries was also in Grove Road, the shop sold home-grown tomatoes etc and was run by dear old Mr Abbiss. Browns, Water Lane, they had a bakery at the side of their little shop and home, Sid Brown was the baker, Olive Brown came round each day with bread in a big basket, in winter she had a sack round her shoulders like a shawl... Bertha Brown ran the little shop where I was sent to buy sugar, vinegar, salt etc. for my mum, behind the shop was a little room where old Mrs Brown lived, the shop is still there in Water Lane'.

Right: Postcard published by H Odell, some time after 1907 when the bell tower was added to the church. The horse trough complete with gas lamp is surely a more pleasing sight than today's mini-roundabout.
Below: View of Grove Road between the wars.

HITCHIN, ROMAN CATHOLIC CHURCH.

Above: 81 Grove Road (circa 1908) next door but one to the Nursery Garden. From left to right: 'Harry, Jack (my favourite brother) and myself (Nellie Charles). Next door on the right was the undertaker, his wife was a nurse who was very fond of Harry and if he didn't eat his dinner he'd nip next door. If he tore his trousers, which he invariably did, she'd mend them before he got home.'
Left: Second World War pillbox on the north east side of the railway bridge.

FLORENCE STREET

The origins of Taylors Lane (later Florence Street) marked but not named on the 1818 Plan of the Town and Parish of Hitchin, are unknown. The street is still known as Taylors Lane on the 1886 Ordnance Survey map. The lane became Florence Street by 1900 and celebrates Florence Nightingale whose fame dates from the Crimean War (1854 - 56).

The street leads from Nightingale Road down into what was Ransom's cow meadows. In the 1940's Alderman's Dairies, just beyond the vets in Grove Road, had a bridge across the Hiz where cows would have been led from grazing to milking, prior to the construction of the recreation ground. The oldest property in the street is the thatched cottage on the left, at a slightly lower level than the modern road and perched above the river. This must surely be Hitchin's only remaining thatched cottage and for as long as anyone can remember there has been a Pilkington living in this attractive cottage.

A substantial building, which is frequently obscured by large removal vans or 'pantechnicons', as their horse-drawn predecessors would have been called, is the old Salvation Army Barracks. The foundation stone was laid in 1888 in what was at this time still Taylors Lane. Built to cater for a congregation of five hundred it has impressive foundation stones along the front. One of these stones bears the name of Commandant H H Booth, was this perhaps one of the great general's family? It is significant that Hitchin had its barracks only ten years after the foundation of the Salvation Army. The Army flourished in the area until the 1950s and many a bleak Christmas or wet Sunday afternoon has been enlivened by the spirited playing of well-known hymns. A favourite place for the gathering of the Salvation Army Band was on the corner of Kings Road by the side of the old Moss's building. Sometimes Salvationists lodged with local people as they carried on their mission to preach the gospel and effect social work in the poorer districts of the town. The old established firm of Waters Removals now occupies the site.

Until recently there was a row of cottages at right angles to the street, known as Anderson's Row. This was a row of sixteen cottages named after Major Anderson. This being Florence Street he was perhaps of Crimean War fame. The two up and two down houses were built at right angles to the road in a pattern of four, then a passageway, and then another six cottages. There were two pumps for water, one outside 10 and 11 and the other outside number 16. Greta Underwood, (née Titmus), went to live there when she was fourteen. She was born in 1888. This family lived at number 11 Anderson's Row. In 1985 these were all demolished by the Council to make way for a housing development for the elderly which bears the name Anderson House.

A brass plaque inside the dining area of this attractive development reads:–

'This Extra Care Sheltered Housing Scheme for elderly persons was commissioned and designed by North Hertfordshire District Council and formerly opened on the 3 October 1985 by Sir George Young Bt. MP, Parliamentary Under Secretary of State for the Department of the Environment.'

Michael K Tatham,
Chairman of the Council'.

It is interesting to note that Ben Ward, in whose memory this book is dedicated, was born at number 35 Florence Street.

Above: Charles Pilkington and his mother in the early 1920s, in the back garden of Number 20 Florence Street. He was a carpenter and worked for Barkers (the woodyard) and on the railways.
Above right: Charles Pilkington's mother, Ann in the back garden 'evidently she did all the gardening'.
Right: The foundation stone of the Salvation Army Barracks, laid in 1888 and, below, the Barracks in 1995 showing its new function.

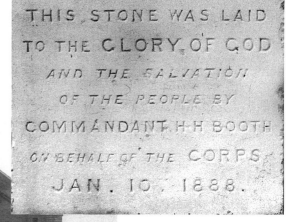

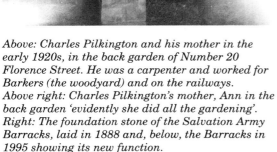

Tiles

Much nineteenth century and early twentieth century urban development took place to satisfy the contemporary demand for living space and for industrial capacity. Hence much of that development was purely functional with little heed paid to variety or flamboyance. Nevertheless, as we have seen elsewhere in this book, evidence of some remarkable attention to detail still remains, not least of which are attractive and colourful tiles and tile patterns in Hitchin.

Messrs Brookers supplied decorative tiles and used the catalogue of Messrs Broad & Company, London, 1910. Present day examples of tiling also occur, for example in the John Myatt shop front in Nightingale Road.

Left and top right: The John Myatt shop was originally built in 1905 for Hitchin grocer W B Moss. The modern tiles maintain the original period style.
Right: A lasting reminder that this company traded here until 1995 (Market Place).

BROAD & CO. LTD., LONDON.

Encaustic Paving.

No. 32   No. 38   No. 35

No. 33   No. 5A   No. 6

No. 40   No. 31   No. 39

Scale :—¾" to a Foot.

ESTIMATES GIVEN AND DESIGNS SUBMITTED FOR ALL KINDS OF TILING.

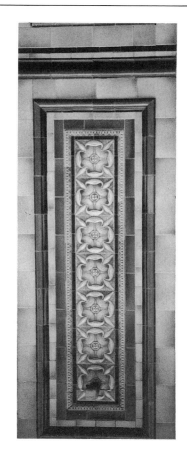

Top left: Tile patterns from Broad & Co of London. The term 'encaustic' describes an early method of making decorative tiles, normally glazed.
Above: Ceramic wall tiles surviving from the 1930s in Tilehouse street.
Below: Front porch floor tiles in a 1909 house in West Hill.

Gas in Hitchin

The gas works were built on a site at Starlings Bridge, known as Benge Mead in 1834. On 8 October that year Hitchin was lit by gas for the first time. To celebrate, the company treated the contractor's workmen to supper at a cost of £9 5s 0d. Originally known as 'The Gas Company' it became the Hitchin Gas Company Limited in 1888. A further site for the manufacture of coal gas was bought from William Ransom in 1896, adjacent to the railway line, near the Cambridge Road bridge. Gas sales boomed until an adequate supply of electricity was assured in 1923. Gas lighting was slowly replaced by its rival. In 1933 the Hitchin Gas Company Ltd was taken over by the expanding Tottenham & District Gas Company Ltd., ending almost a century of local enterprise and control.

In 1949, following the nationalisation of the Gas Industry, Hitchin became part of the Eastern Gas Board. Some houses remained unconverted until the late 1960's, the last town gas lamps being along Charlton Road.

The gas holder was demolished at the Nightingale Road site in the late 1940's and the area continued as a service depot, later to close entirely. It gradually became an eyesore until N & P Windows took over the site and gave it a face-lift. They, too, have gone leaving a motor firm and Ashley Business Centre now occupying the site. Interestingly, earlier this century a Billiard Hall stood as an extension to the gas office near the recreation ground gate.

A SONG OF COMFORT

Who Makes Hot Taps Really Hot ?
Who Puts "Chillspots" On The Spot ?
Who Makes Cooking Mere Child's Play ?
Who Drives Washday Cares Away ?

MR. THERM,
of course !

If you are interested in questions of modern home comfort, you should pay a visit to the Gas Company's Showroom. There you will see for yourself how Mr. Therm can help you to bring your home up-to-date. The attendant will be glad to answer any enquiries you may care to make.

HITCHIN & DISTRICT GAS CO.
STARLINGS BRIDGE, HITCHIN
TELEPHONE **309**

Top left: Behind the baby, we can see the newly-erected gas holder (1934).
Above: Advertisement in 1936/7 Official Guide.
Left: A gas valve cover of the Tottenham and District Gas Company still to be found in Bancroft.

NIGHTINGALE ROAD

Though the name of this road undoubtedly influenced the naming of Florence Street its origins go further back. It is thought that a Nightingale Inn gave its name to the road and it carries similar resonance to Starlings Bridge.

Memories of Nightingale Road in the 1940s and 1950s by Derek Wheeler with earlier recollections by Marshall Dellar and others:

'I have always felt that the connection people make between Florence Street, Nightingale Road and the nursing heroine of Scutari is false. I spent the first twenty years of my life in cottages named Nightingale Cottages and they were, and still are, dated 1844, which was at least a decade before the residents of Hitchin had heard of Miss Nightingale. Either the road, (an extension of Silver Street on old maps) gave its name to the cottages or the cottages gave their name to the road. In those days the cottages backed onto land owned by the Ransom family.

Nightingale Road was a thriving thoroughfare, populated by small shopkeepers and railway workers and their families. Most of the neighbours in the forties and fifties attended St Saviour's Church, as it was then known and their children attended either St Saviour's School in Radcliffe Road, or, like myself, Wilshere Dacre. There were two other schools close by, the Sacred Heart Convent in Verulam Road and St Michael's College on what is now the Police Station site.

My grandfather, Frank Arthur Wheeler, had established a florist's, greengrocery, nursery and seedsman's shop on the corner of King's Road where John Myatt's music shop now stands. F A Wheeler had this shop built in 1925 on land which, I believe, had been a timber yard. Before that he had worked from a shop on the corner of Garden Row. He worked land in Whinbush Road, Benslow Lane and, during the war years, along Bedford Road near the New Inn at Holwell. The business thrived on rose growing and my father's brother, Bob Wheeler, recently retired from running his own nursery business in Benslow Lane. Frank Arthur used to judge at Rose and Chrysanthemum Shows in the neighbourhood and could be seen round the town on a battered motorcycle held together with florist wire. My father, Frank Carrington Wheeler, ran the shop side of the business until it ceased trading on the death of F A Wheeler in the early 1960's.

Surprisingly, there were three other greengrocers in the road; Rainbow's opposite what is now the vets; Gregory's nearer Garden Row and John Howard on the corner of Radcliffe Road. While the vets is mentioned, this is allegedly the oldest building in the road, being the former home of Cox the newsagent who worked opposite. The cottages next to the vet's share the same building line and ground level as Nightingale Cottages further up.

There were plenty of grocers too. W B Moss had a wonderful shop where John Myatt's brass premises are now. It had mahogany counters, large canisters painted in pretty blues and gold concealing exotic teas, bacon and a red painted bacon slicer. There were Bentwood chairs for elderly customers to rest on while placing their orders (which would be delivered later), and a cash office where a lady sat surrounded by metal spikes on which she impaled orders and receipts. The grocery counter on the left was presided over by Mr Winters and the bacon counter on the right had Mr Backhurst in charge. To the rear of the shop and in the cellar could be seen Bob West, a well-known local bee-keeper, trundling tea chests and sacks on a barrow. Biscuits were on display at waist height in glass-topped tins and sugar was scooped out into blue 'sugar paper' bags. Balls of string and brown paper were visible on the grocery counter for

This view, taken c1912, is clearly recognisable today. The pillar box has gone and the trader's names have changed. The telegraph pole stands close to what later became Furr's Wet Fish Shop.

wrapping purchases. Moss's had a fleet of delivery bicycles and also a van or two, which were kept at the rear of the building.

The Co-op had a big store, Hitchin's first self-service shop, where Studman & Morgan's premises are now. Opposite this Miss Ivy Roach, an elderly lady who habitually wore blue mittens, ran a grocery shop. It was heated in the winter by a black 'Valor' paraffin stove which cast circles of smelly light onto the ceiling. Her counter was like a theatre set with Ivy as the sole performer. The 'proscenium arch' was formed by biscuit tins, cornflake packets, stacked tins of Batchelors or Benedict peas, all of which almost reached the ceiling and bridged over the counter with coloured cardboard advertisements for Peak Freans or Brasso. She had another counter which had glass display cabinets containing Pond's cold cream, still in wartime packaging. Her mother ran a shoe shop next door and when Mrs Roach died Ivy continued to run both shops. The luckless shoe purchaser would have to take the routine turn in the grocery queue and then wait whilst Ivy shut her own shop, disappeared out the back where no customer had ever been, only to re-appear to unlock the shoe shop from inside, leaving other customers waiting on the doorstep! On closing the shop in the evening she would load cardboard boxes of goods into her ancient Lanchester car and make deliveries around the area. She was one of the few lady drivers in the area and allegedly one of the slowest! There were at least two other grocers shops towards the Woolpack pub.

Shoes could be repaired by Mr Thorogood who worked in premises next to Cherry's. Newspapers could be bought at Cox's, which was in the same row of shops as Ivy Roach's. There were four butchers in the road, Proctor & Doling's opposite the vets, Marsom's further down, the Co-op butchery department opposite the Woolpack and Mrs Smoothy's opposite Nightingale Cottages.

Mrs Smoothy had a slaughter house up the yard. All sorts of farm animals would be delivered to the yard gate and released across the pavement, behind hurdles, to meet their fate up the yard. The gutter here used to run with blood and animal effluent. Sometimes the animals would be herded from the station by a drover, in among the traffic. Occasionally they were accompanied by 'Allah', a well-known Hitchin character. He was usually resident at the cattle market on market days or as a mascot for the football team on Saturdays. He dressed in wellingtons, a cloth cap and an army greatcoat fastened with string. Brian Limbrick recalls his policeman father speaking of 'Allah' sleeping rough in the poultry market. Sometimes the pigs escaped and skipped off down the road, to be chased back from the Woolpack to the consternation of motorists and to the delight of small children!

Opposite Florence Street there were, as now, many shops; butchers, various confectioners' occupying a shop known as the 'Red Shop', at one time an antique shop called Burnett's and a high-class gents' outfitters. Penton & Dean sold traditional suits, school uniforms and Bukta scout equipment. This shop later became the home of Worbey & Kingsley, electrical contractors, who are still with us elsewhere in the town. Outside this shop stood one of the many bus stops in the road.

On the opposite side of the road, on the corner of Florence Street, there was a grocer's with a brick pillarbox outside. Then came a tobacconists, followed by Furr's wet fish shop. Having mentioned the Co-op butchery already, we come to the old premises of Nott's bakery shop and Mr Whittaker the chemist. He would only dispense private prescriptions, no National Health nonsense for him! Next came Mrs Williams' haberdashery and corset shop. It was said that she wore a wig because her fuzzy black hair, loaded with hair pins, always looked the same whenever you saw her! By the bridge over the Hiz stood Dunkinson's sweet shop where ice cream (Eldorado I think) could be bought.

On the corner of Whinbush and Verulam Roads stood the corrugated structure of the Trades & Labour Club much altered to modern standards in recent years.

Above: Waiting for the procession! An A E Lupton postcard issued to commemorate the coronation of George V in 1911.
Right and below left: Two views of Garden Row, sixty years apart.
Below right: Attractive bootscraper from Nightingale Road.

The Woolpack – Starlings Bridge

The Woolpack was built about 1840 by W Foss who was a woolsorter. The London Company of Woolmen or Woolpackers, whose emblem is the 'woolpack', was founded around 1300 and exercised considerable powers. In the seventeenth century it was compulsory for all woolcombers to be licensed by the Company. In the House of Lords the judges used to sit on woolsacks. It is alleged that these woolpacks were intended not merely for comfort but to remind the public that wool was a main source of our national wealth. The Lord Chancellor's seat is still called the Woolsack.

Hitchin's parish church, St Mary's, is what is called a 'wool church', that is to say the present building, in the main, was erected from donations given by well-to-do merchants in the town, who had made their money from the valuable trade in wool which existed in the Middle Ages. A woolstapler's mark can be seen on the left-hand side of the south porch.

The Woolpack had a lovely orchard and gardens adjacent to the River Hiz where generations of children picked fruit; there was a smithy in the yard run by Mr Berridge which was still standing until the late 1940's, the last working forge in Hitchin. In later years the pub was presided over by characters called Dolly and Cyril Bostock. It had been, like the 'Leicester', a Fordham's pub. In cottages adjacent to the pub could be found Hitchin's Red Cross Centre, where electrical massage was given for muscular problems. There was the gas works and showrooms at Starlings Bridge, the gasholder was still there in the late forties, adjacent to the River Hiz, and could be seen over the roof of the Woolpack.

There were three hairdressers; a 'ladies' trading under the exotic name of 'Madame Bettina', had an upstairs room in her house as a salon. Locals knew her as just Betty Spary, a native of the north. Mr Trussell, opposite Cherry's, doubled as a barber and proprietor of a toyshop cum dolls hospital. This was a front-room shop conversion; no fancy glass plate windows for him, he still had gas lighting well into the fifties. Fred Rivenell cut hair further up the road near the junction with Radcliffe Road. He knew everything! His sight went in later years and it was a bit frightening to be inches away from potential blood-letting! His shop was sandwiched between the smells of Furr's fish and chip shop and John Howard's greengrocery.

Further up the road had stood, from 1912, the Herts & Beds Farmers Co-Operative Bacon Factory. At the front, white-coated staff in tiled surroundings with sawdust on the floor served the pork products. At the rear of the building, brown warehouse coats and wellington boots represented the workers who slaughtered the pigs. Squeals and smells emanated throughout the year from this building and in the summer months it was wise to keep the windows shut! The gutters ran with blood and pig effluent here too.

The road had two garages, both of which sold petrol across the pavement. George Ansell's, (formerly Issot's) and Cherry's, which is still with us. They combine road haulage and ironmongery with their garage business and must be unique in the town as their petrol pumps still cross the pavement. Ansell's were still selling paraffin from a street dispenser in the 1950's. Brown Brothers' Vindec bicycles could be bought at Ansell's. Old ladies used to take their pre-mains accumulator batteries there for charging so they could continue to listen to the BBC Home Service or the Light Programme on their wireless sets.

On the corner of Radcliffe Road there is now, as then, a pub known to generations as The Gloster or later The Gloucester Arms. Even now its name has been changed. Next to this stood another cycle-cum-radio shop, owned by Taberner, later John Gilbert of Baldock. This is where some people in the road bought their first Ecko or Cossor television set so that they could watch the black and white pictures of the Coronation of Queen Elizabeth II. New neighbours and friends were made in 1953 when most of the road gathered round the few television sets, with their thick lenses, which were then 'in situ' to magnify the pictures!

There was a plumber called Bert Sayer, who had premises opposite the lane leading to

Above: Nightingale Road, looking towards The Woolpack, Cox's Newsagents can be seen. Below: The Bacon Factory in 1913. The site is now occupied by an office block.

Finest
ENGLISH PICKLES

SPECIALLY PREPARED FOR
HERTS & BEDS
BACON FACTORY LTD
HITCHIN.

Entered at Stationers Hall

Midland Cottages; his little shop front jutted out beyond the building line. He went to work either on his bicycle or, like many in those days, pushed the tools and materials of his trade in a handcart. At the top of this lane stood the water tower of the old Midland Railway Company, Hitchin's alternative rail connection which passed via Ickleford to Henlow, Bedford and Leicester. This route gave its name to the former title of the Nightingale pub, The Leicester Railway Inn. On the other side of the lane stood a turntable where steam locomotives used to be manually reversed. The large yard, which is still there opposite B & Q's, contained loco sheds and coal dumps with offices belonging to such firms as Bailey, Hawkins, Spicer, Pierson and Franklin. The town weighbridge was in the yard as was Franklin's Corn, Seed and Animal Food Warehouse. Towards the end of World War Two, Williams had a scrap metal dump in the yard and my father, Frank Wheeler, used to get aluminium and perspex from crashed Heinkels and Messerschmitts in order to make me toys at a time when such luxuries were difficult to buy.

The site of B & Q's was originally where Bowman's Flour Mill and the Railway Junction Inn once stood. According to Mr Dellar, the landlord of the Junction pub, Archie Cotton, also traded as a painter and decorator in the town. When the pub closed down Bowman's used the premises as their rest room and canteen.

Nightingale Road was once a self-contained community where almost any commodity could be bought without a walk into town. It had a taxi firm, six bus stops along its length and effectively two railway stations at the end. There were four pubs altogether and a public toilet at the junction with Ickleford Road. In the forties there was still much animal traffic in the road. Circuses on Butts Close sometimes used to march their elephants from the cattle dock at the railway station down Nightingale Road, a rare sight for a child to see. Horses were still a mode of transport. Pierson's, the coal merchants, had stables near Midland Cottages. (These burned down in about 1947

and have been replaced by garages). Their drays could be seen, as could those of the railway and those of Carter Patterson. A man named Hall, who wore a red and white spotted neckerchief, used to drive one of the waggons. The Council used to have a cart which was used for leaf clearance, likewise road makers had a horse-drawn water cart. Gypsy caravans owned by the Loveridge family used to pass by. Wallace's dairy had horse floats, our milkman Fred Ansell used to brake his float by tying a leather sheathed chain round the spokes of a back wheel, while he delivered our milk from a metal crate. The milk bottles had cardboard tops. There were also horse floats from Arnsby's Dairy, Radcliffe Road and from Alderman's in Grove Road.

The main traffic was cycles, hundreds of them, since people used to regularly cycle to work in Letchworth. Many came in from the villages and left their bikes either at the station or with local residents for the day, if they were commuting to Welwyn Garden City or London. Stevenage was only just then becoming industrialised. There was employment nearer at hand. George King's factory in Walsworth Road employed dozens of people, as did Bowman's, the railway itself, the gasworks in Cambridge Road and Sharman's boilerworks also in Cambridge Road. Occasionally steam vehicles were seen on the roads, the Council had a steamroller, Sharman's boilerworks repaired engines and Thurston's hauled their fairground rides to Butts Close behind a steam engine. Simpson's Baldock Brewery delivered beer to the 'Gloster' with a beautiful Sentinel S4 steam lorry until the Suez Crisis. This latter vehicle is now preserved in Norfolk as a bus!

Very few people had cars in the road. Mr Cherry had an Armstrong Siddeley which had a distinctive whine from its 'fluid flywheel', so did Mr and Mrs Burrows who ran a taxi business from a house opposite Ransoms Rec. They wore special chauffeur's livery and at a time when most private cars were black their fleet was an electric green. There were few lady drivers at this time, Mrs Burrows was one, Mrs Wesley in Walsworth, who drove a big

Left: Mrs Priscilla Ayres and her niece Beatrice at the gate of their family home early in the century.

Right: Cows returning to their field in Verulam Road (1930s). Below: Starlings Bridge, c1912.

Austin taxi was another, and Mrs Woodbridge the corsetière from Spirella in Letchworth was another. Mr Whittaker the chemist had a distinctive fawn Austin with a canvas hood, Mr Rumbelow the insurance agent had a little Standard and 'Chiefy' Bostock at the Woolpack had a succession of Austin Sevens which he kept well after their 'sell by' date. Cherry's had a fleet of lorries for their road haulage business and Bowman's had a fleet of Albions in a distinctive cream and red livery, one of which is still preserved at Ickleford.

There was constant noise and bustle from the G P O sorting office who shared premises with the telephone engineers in Kings Road. The building continues in use as the Hitchin Auction Rooms. Train whistles and the bang and crash of shunting trucks could be heard day and night. This was mixed with the sound of squealing pigs from the Bacon Factory. On a good day Ransom's distillery and Russell's tanyard wafted odours across the town, gently enhanced with the fragrances from Garratt & Cannon's sweet factory. On a bad day the Bacon Factory used to out-do everyone's efforts with the 'Airwick' bottle!

Time was marked at one o'clock by Russell's lunchtime hooter and excitement was encouraged by the occasional wail of the fire siren in Paynes Park calling the Brigade into action. One of the local sights was to see fireman Ralph French dash out of his building firm in Whinbush Road and be in time to leap onto the old Dennis 'Ace' fire engine as it came round the Woolpack corner. He would don his helmet and tunic as the engine sped up towards the railway station. I remember a chimney fire in Nightingale Cottages on Christmas Eve 1947 when the 'Dennis' arrived to douse the remains of my mother's straw hat. The machine was accompanied by a policeman on his bicycle to control the onlookers and a bill arrived some days later for calling out the brigade.

On a Sunday the only sounds to be heard were the occasional train, birdsong, maybe a bus and the seemingly one phrase of St Saviour's Church bells. In the evening it was so quiet that you could hear the clock striking at the Priory, always slightly adrift from Greenwich Mean Time. That peace has gone forever!

Mrs Priscilla Arnold (née Ayres) born in 1905, lived at 107 Nightingale Road in her youth and has vivid memories of the life there earlier in the century:

'...the cellar was down steps. It had six bedrooms and belonged to Mr Ansell who had a butcher's shop on the corner of Periwinkle Lane. He used to serve my mother... you could buy a joint of beef for five pence a pound. A young couple got married and came and lived with us, they had two rooms at the back.....she was Mrs Atherton, she was the first lady to go down in a parachute in France from an Irving's 'chute. That was in 1930, she worked there.

...there was a big orchard down the bottom (of the garden).... and the greengrocer used to buy a plum, a pear and an apple tree from my mother and then he came into the garden whenever he wanted to pick them to sell 'em and we weren't allowed to touch the fruit on those three trees..... a schoolboy used to come with a basket every morning and pick up the fallers to sell them a-penny-a-pound in the greengrocery shop. It was a Mr King.'

The 'Flu Epidemic of 1918

'...my brother died December 1918. You took a person to the Church to bury them and when you came back someone else in the house had died...'cos you all had deep black them days and my mother had three dresses made for us three girls and I think five different families wore those dresses within the first twelve months of us having them...and of course we lost Dad as well in 1917 at Ypres'.

Matchboxes

Up until recent years it was the practice of shops and Public Houses to have specially printed labels, to advertise their premises and wares, put on the matchboxes which they sold.

This was a cheap way of making the public aware of their services in the days when many people smoked cigarettes or pipes.

Booklet matches are still used as an advertising medium by restaurants and hotels to give away to customers and to a large extent have superseded the traditional matchbox for advertising.

RANSOM'S RECREATION GROUND

This area of land, bounded as it is by the railway, Nightingale Road, King's and Alexandra Roads and Grove Road can still be imagined as grazing land. Children from the surrounding houses had probably played on this land for generations (unofficially) as Mr Matthews of Baldock recalls:-

'When I first remember it, it was a milking farm, the farmer was named Camps. When he left it was taken over by brothers named Lee and we used to play cricket in the meadows. Lee used to think we would damage the land since his cows were feeding there and he would drive us off. We went off to the lime bank out of his way until he'd disappeared and then we would return. One or two young men used the upper field for golf with a few holes marked out with flags. There was a pond in the middle but this was soon to go'.

Mrs Arnold remembers the opening in 1929 as an official Recreation Ground. She was living in a balconied house in Nightingale Road:–

'They had the small band and three men came into the bedroom and stood on the balcony and spoke to the people below, they thanked Mr Francis Ransom for giving it to the town'.

The pond went as the Hitchin Urban District Council took over the land, changing rooms, the contemporary 'Wicksteed' green-painted swings, roundabout, see-saw and brass-bottomed slide were erected. Many short-trousered bottoms must have been worn out on this slide and teeth removed by the swinging plank of the see-saw. Athletic youths would swing from the end bars of the see-saw frame and cover their hands with thick black grease. In latter years as the nation has become more safety-conscious the area has become a fenced, dog-free 'adventure playground' and very attractive it looks too.

Football and cricket are both played in this 'rec' and Mr Matthews remembers that Barkers the timber merchants and Willmotts the builders had inter-firm matches which were played on this ground. Occasionally the fire brigade held competitions here against the backdrop of Midland Cottages. Vertical targets were erected, competing crews had to knock them down with their powerful jets, against the clock. There is another fire brigade connection with the ground; the wartime National Fire Service had its local headquarters in the small brick building between the Hiz and Grove Road. Until fairly recently the Hitchin & District Society of Model Engineers occupied this building and the remains of their small railway track can still be seen adjacent to it. A generation of local children can remember being given rides on the miniature steam locomotive. Nicola and Robert Douglas remember the miniature train in the early 1970's '...the seats were just little ones, you sat astride them like a bench...there was always a driver with a flat cap on and dirty blue overalls, all grubby... The trains were more fun than the swings'.

A unique picture of Ransom's 'Rec' remains in the main corridor at Strathmore Infants' School, the first generation of children who attended this school in the late 1940's can remember it being painted. A later generation had it concealed from view, and the present generation can see what the steam railway and children's fashions were like in 1949.

It is amazing that the local authority could even think of disposing of a part of this local amenity for a housing development in the recent past, and yet a public outcry and press campaign had to be undertaken to prevent this happening. The council of Mr Ransom's day had no such intentions.

Right: Jean Renwick soon after the 'Rec' opened.
Below: The brass-bottomed 'Wicksteed' slide in the 1930s.
Bottom: The roundabout and seesaw. In the background can be seen the Hitchin to Bedford train, axed as part of the Beeching Plan in the 1960s.

HITCHIN AND THE GREAT NORTHERN RAILWAY

'The Railways afford great accommodation to travellers, who can go to any part of England from this station. The Great Northern has a first-class station here; the Cambridge Railway, which is leased to the Great Northern Railway Company, runs in here; and the Midland has a goods station, and passengers by that line arrive and depart from the Great Northern Platform. Omnibuses and flys are announced to meet every train, and flys and cabs may be had at the Railway Inn, adjoining the station, and from the Sun Hotel.'

Taken from a Hitchin Handbook of 1875

Hitchin was already an important market town for corn, cattle and sheep, and provisions before the coming of the railway; it was one of most populous towns in Hertfordshire. Only twenty years after the opening of the world's first public railway, the Stockton and Darlington, was a London to York mainline through Hitchin considered. Work began on the successor scheme, the Great Northern Railway, in 1847 and today it forms part of the East Coast mainline from London to Edinburgh. The arrival of the first train in August 1850 marked an important new chapter in the town's development. Its influences still persist today. Even so Jack Simmons opens his *The Railway in Town and Country* (1986) by noting that 'Local historians sometimes go to great lengths to avoid the treatment of railways'. Reginald Hine, whose *History of Hitchin* is one of the most interesting accounts yet written of a small English town, gives a full chapter to coaches and then, after the briefest possible mention of railways, abandons them to figure in a chronological table at the end of his book.

Queen Victoria's eight minute stop at Hitchin Station in 1851

August 27 1851

'My wife and daughters Emma and Juliana and I set off in the open carriage for Hitchin at twenty minutes past twelve and arrived there at two. We had to make our way through a great crowd to get to the platform of the Great Northern station where, on presenting our ticket, we were admitted to a very good place on a reserved part of the platform. At ten minutes past three the Royal Saloon Carriage containing the Queen, Prince Albert and three of the Royal children stopped exactly opposite us. We had a very good sight of them, Prince Albert drawing the curtain away from the window and the Queen and himself standing up in the carriage, appearing pleased with the decoration of the station and the immense assemblage of the principal inhabitants and also of the population extending a long way on the banks of the cutting of the railroad. After staying about eight minutes for a supply of water during which God Save the Queen was sung, and loud huzzas saluted the ear of the Queen, a few moments pause took place, and a young lady (Miss Exton), one of the Society of Friends, presented the Queen with a small plateau of beautiful flowers which were most graciously accepted'.

NB: Miss Exton was the daughter of a Hitchin banker whose firm were local bankers of the Great Northern Rail.

An entry from 'A Chronicle of Small Beer' The Early Victorian Diaries of a Hertfordshire Brewer'. Gerald Curtis. Published by Phillimore in 1970

Hitchin's first passenger service initially included twelve trains to London on weekdays, the fastest reaching Kings Cross in forty-four minutes, about the same time that it takes a semi-fast service to reach the capital today.

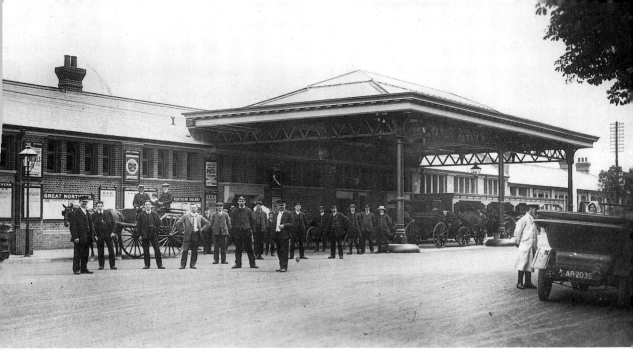

*Top: Some things never change! Waiting for the homecoming traveller
at the front entrance of the Great Northern Railway Station.
Above: Note the large contingent of railway staff on the 'down' platform.
Right: GNR water stopcock cover.*

Literally overnight the town became more accessible to a much wider range of influences. The grain trade was boosted, drawing the town's traditional hinterland of North Hertfordshire and South Bedfordshire, and the new Corn Exchange (which opened in 1853) brought traders and ancillary dealers from as far afield as Liverpool and Stourbridge.

The passenger service soon encouraged Hitchin's first railway commuters who could now travel daily to and from London with relative ease. These, in turn, led to building on land between the town centre and the new railway station; this area became so popular for residential development that it soon recorded some of the highest land prices seen to date in the town. It also provided, through good links with Cambridge, the basis for Hitchin's important place in the history of female education in the United Kingdom; in 1869 a Ladies College opened in Benslow House in association with the University of Cambridge. The college was located here because, apart from good rail links, the town offered a healthy rural environment away from the dangers of male undergraduate company. After 1873 the establishment did move to Cambridge to become Girton (alas not Hitchin) College. Today the Station Bungalow, at one time a Lodge for Benslow House, serves as a reminder of all those young ladies moving to and from Cambridge by rail in search of their education.

Railway services also brought railway time! Mrs Nellie Coxall (née Charles) born 1900 remembers:-

'My father was on the railways... he was doing twelve hours a day, six in the morning until six at night, or six at night until six in the morning.... so we moved to the Station Cottages, the one nearest the railway... the garden went right down to the railway. My father was an Inspector then, and at the other end was the Inspector for the trains...of course, you had knockers-up in those days ... when you were on duty in the night the drivers, they couldn't depend on the clocks, they'd knock them up.

My father came home one dinner time to have his dinner and it wasn't ready, and he said to my mother 'where's my dinner?' and she said 'well, I put the vegetables on by the 12.20', and he said 'yes! but it was late'!

We went to bed by the 9.20 - mother would say 'there goes the 9.20 - time for bed'...and we got up by the 6.30.

... and if there was an accident a pram-like contraption was kept at the bottom of our garden and if anybody came we all raced to see. And it was pushed... if the person was dead or alive it was pushed all the way up to the hospital because there was no other means. They hadn't got an ambulance in those days ...and I always remember, one man was killed and his head came off, and my father had to put him into this thing ...and all the children ran down to have a look at the head. But of course it had been put in the pram. My father couldn't eat his dinner that day. It was one of the workmen who was crushed on the line, he didn't see the train coming. This 'ambulance', it was just like a long pram with a hood and cover. It was kept in the shed at the bottom of the garden, and if we saw the doors open, we'd be there! You know, children are like that.'

Goods traffic was of crucial importance to the GNR and an important yard was established on Nightingale Road and a wide variety of goods passed through it. Some, such as coal and timber, were already in use locally but they now became cheaper and more reliable; others, such as different building materials like Welsh slate, were new and they changed the way things were done in the town. Hitchin's importance as a railway centre was quickly reinforced by the opening of the line to Shepreth (in October 1850) and then Cambridge and, between 1857-69, the town was briefly a mainline junction when the Midland Railway built its line from Leicester to Hitchin, so that it could gain access to London at Kings Cross in advance of the completion of its own terminal at St Pancras.

Even today there are still reminders of the earliest days of the railway in the town if you look closely. A portion of the station itself on the 'up' (London) side dates from 1850 as do the original block of railway cottages overlooking today's yard and car park. The booking hall retains its lettered stone entrance doorways from the substantial rebuilding undertaken in 1910-11 when the 'new' station master's house also appeared and there are several stopcock covers with the GNR markings around the station. A plan of 1907 shows the range of outbuildings north-east of the station adjacent to Cambridge Road and still in use by maintenance staff as a mess room, stores and shops for a plumber, gas fitter, a carpenter, a smith and the signal fitters. A little further away, on Cambridge Road, one of the GNR's boundary markers also survives and, off Nightingale Road, Midland Cottages, a fence made of some very old sleepers and bull head rail and some small houses called Leicester Cottages remind us of the railway legacy. The goods yard, which also provided a home to the separate Midland Railway engine shed, still retains some interesting if dilapidated buildings; very regrettably the Midland engine shed was gratuitously demolished only recently.

Further afield still is the house off Highbury Road, originally called Hillside, but now part of the Caldicott Centre, which was for a time the home of Richard Johnson, Chief Engineer of the GNR. Johnson was also the driving force behind the Mission on Walsworth Road which predated the Baptist Church; the iron Mission Hall itself still survives as the Liberal Club in Stotfold!

Hitchin's railway past is still an influence on its present. The town remains the junction of the Cambridge Branch and a depot for infrastructure maintenance and will soon become a north London interchange for the new Royal Mail rail collection service. Also many of those who commute today from the 'Poets' estate (actually built on portions of the Purwell Field) might not realise they are living on land that once belonged to GNR who hoped to build more marshalling yards and a locomotive works on it. If this had come about perhaps Hitchin might have had an industrial railway history more like that of Doncaster!

Below: The 'new' station master's house.
Bottom: Contemporary view of Midland Cottages built in the 1850s especially for employees of the Midland Railway.

Lavender Growing in Hitchin

'In each bright drop there is a spell
Tis from the soil we love so well
From English gardens won.'

This delightful rhyme appeared on all labels of lavender water distilled for sale to the public at the former chemist shop belonging to Perks & Llewellyn in Hitchin's High Street. According to tradition the business was founded in 1790 but it was not until about 1822 that Edward Perks began cultivating lavender commercially. By 1876 when his son, Samuel, was in charge, there were about thirty five acres of land outside the town devoted to lavender, which yielded sufficient oil to produce two thousand gallons of lavender water.

Samuel Perks showed at a number of international exhibitions. He obtained an Honourable Mention in the London Exhibition of 1862 for '...goodness of quality lavender oil', in Paris three years later he secured the only Prize Medal for lavender water and at Philadelphia in 1876 a medal, diploma and report.

In 1907, by which time Perks & Llewellyn had been acquired by Richard Lewis, the suffragette Sylvia Pankhurst came to Hitchin on a fashion assignment for the London Evening News when she declared: 'Lavender water is falling on evil days'.

Her words had a ring of truth about them. Lavender water was no longer in great demand but it was not until 1961 that the last proprietor, Mr Lewis's daughter, Violet Lewis, closed down the business. Lavender growing, however, continued until the early 1970's.

However Violet Lewis had the foresight to retain many of the shop's fixtures, together with much of the material that

A postcard of 1941 showing (left to right) F M Lewis, B Edmunds, H Massam, V E Lewis and F Hide picking lavender in Perks and Llewellyn's fields.

Charming interior view of Perks and Llewellyn's shop in the High Street, now faithfully reproduced in Hitchin Museum.

had made Perks & Llewellyn famous in Victorian times. She set up a museum by re-erecting the greater part of the shop and its furnishings in a purpose built extension to her home off Lucas Lane and opening the display to the public by appointment.

Subsequently she generously donated it all to the Hertfordshire Medical & Pharmaceutical Museum Trust. After several years of fund raising the trustees were able to transfer everything to Hitchin Museum where the shop interior and its fascinating contents were again reconstructed. These together with a specially laid out physic garden in the museum grounds, were officially opened by Professor Harold Ellis in 1990.

Perks & Llewellyn were by no means the only lavender distillers in Hitchin. By 1850 William Ransom, the founder of Wm Ransom & Son, the pharmaceutical chemists in Bancroft, was already known as a cultivator and distiller of lavender. This practice is continued to this day although the lavender is no longer grown locally.

Yet another lavender manufacturer was T J Martin of Sun Street who produced 'Royal Hitchin' lavender water in the last years of Victoria's reign.

WHINBUSH ROAD

Whinbush (or Wimbush) is an alternative name for the gorse or furze plant. Built on Great Wimbush field, the Whinbush Grove side of the road was developed more than the opposite side (which was not an open field), though in living memory there were cottages where the flats now stand. As the houses were constructed along Whinbush Road, the strips of land attached to the Grove's houses were gradually shortened.

Wimbush Lane (as Whinbush Road was) is not named on the 1818 Plan of Hitchin and though by 1844 it is recorded as Whinbush Lane it reverts to Wimbush Lane on a map of 1851. George Beaver, a nineteenth century Hitchin surveyor, is still calling it Whinbush Lane in 1844. He does refer to it as Whinbush Road by 1892. By the early 1900s it is definitely Whinbush Road. It is because it was simply a lane that it is so narrow at its entrance near the lodge end. It seems to have been widened in the 1880s.

Derrick Else remembers:

'I was born at No. 59 Whinbush Road and lived there in the 1920s and '30s.

Approaching from Nightingale Road the east side of the road is remarkably unchanged. On the other side almost everything, houses, cottages, businesses, allotments have all gone. The new buildings, dominated by the Council flats development in the sixties, serve as a sharp contrast between old and new, as do the scores of cars now lining the street compared with the half dozen or so that I remember.

At the junction of Whinbush Road and Verulam Road stood the old Trades and Labour Club, a popular venue offering billiards, snooker, bar, et cetera attended by many local men (not ladies I recall) including railwaymen from the then thriving passenger goods and engineering departments at the other end of Nightingale Road.

The next three houses, Nos. 78, 79 and 80, are still as I recall them. Next at No. 81 stood the office, yard and workshop of William French, builder, undertaker and shopfitter still there today after several occupations and currently offering car sales and service. Across the road the large family house was built by Charles French in the 1830s. Pat French recalls an early map on which it is the only house in the locality beside a stream running through green pastures! When Charles' son William died in 1928 his sons, Charles and Ralph carried on the business while their sister, May, kept house for them.

Both brothers were volunteer firemen and can be seen in photographs of the old Hitchin Fire Brigade whose headquarters was then in Paynes Park. I can remember the bell in the house ringing to summon them to a fire and hearing Ralph roar off on his motorcycle.

The gas lamp which stood near French's yard was a popular meeting place for boys, especially on dark evenings, exchanging and playing with cigarette cards and marbles. At No. 82 Stanley Lee had his electrical business in what might be seen as the pioneering days of electricity and wireless for the home. Norman Johnson recalls working for him on a contract at Bygrave, reporting at 7.30am in Whinbush Road, loading his bicycle with tools, cable, switches etc. and cycling to Bygrave and back each day.

The houses from thereon to Walsworth Road are very much the same as in old photographs. At Whinbush Grove the corner premises were occupied by J Day, decorator (the gates to his yard in Whinbush Road can still be seen). Mrs Day ran a small grocery and provision shop. This was invaluable to people, like my mother, who shopped only when things were actually needed. With so many shops in Nightingale Road there was no problem from Monday to Saturday but on Sunday every shop and store throughout the town was closed. Mrs Day

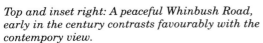

Top and inset right: A peaceful Whinbush Road, early in the century contrasts favourably with the contempory view.
Above: Wash-house, still standing in the garden of Number 102, which was built by Jeeves in 1875.
Right: Derek Wheeler and David Milne making coal briquettes using coal dust and cement in 1946.

could not break the law by opening the shop but she would help those who needed the odd packet of tea or butter or sugar. I was often despatched to go quickly and quietly and knock at Mr Day's big gates to be served by Mrs Day at the back door! Two other people on that side of the road I seem to remember. Around No. 100 lived the 'faggot lady', who sold hot faggots and delicious gravy which I collected in a large jug, usually for supper.

In what was then No. 121 Mr Warren, Stonemason, had his business in a yard which also contained some small cottages. My father did some carting for Mr Warren, probably with a horse and cart and later with his Ford lorry. Beyond, at the junction with Walsworth Road, still stands the unique house (thatched in my time, now tiled) and home of the Cannon family of sweet factory fame. As a boy at Hitchin Boys' Grammar School I can remember the delicious odours that floated over the wall by the North Court.

Returning to Nightingale Road and proceeding up the west side of Whinbush Road there was Mr Berridge the blacksmith. Although I daresay his address was in Nightingale Road we always regarded him as at 'the bottom of the road'. Next, four or five cottages and French's wood yard, storing all sorts of timber for house building and use in their workshop across the road. Next their large old house, No. 60 and No. 60a (Johnson).

At No. 59 my father and mother ran a laundry business. Earlier my father also had several horses and carriages used mainly I think for funerals. The large stables and carriage shed, including two old carriages, remained mouldering for many years. One stable only was in use, housing 'Joey' a big old horse kept in honourable retirement after my father purchased a model 'T' Ford lorry, one of only half a dozen vehicles in the road. I can still see the horse brasses, collars, harnesses, brushes, combs, et cetera hanging in the empty stables. Wherever did they go? In the 1914 Trade Directory, my father appears as 'Laundry Proprietor'.

Proceeding 'up the road' several more cottages (close to the road but with long gardens at the rear extending right to the River Hiz). On this side also Messrs Abbiss and Wheeler, both well known local nurserymen, had their large outdoor nurseries, again extending to that natural water supply the Hiz. Mr Abbiss, whose premises were in Grove Road, was also well known as a gymnastic instructor at the old gymnasium in Brand Street and he could be seen riding his bicycle, back stiff and straight, many years later.

Further up the road, the houses 'Hawkswick' and 'St Andrews' built by the Masters family still remain, although Mr Masters' yard and all the allotments alongside were overtaken by the Ransom's development. Sam Masters recalls his father describing how he provided horses and carts working on the building of RAF Henlow Camp.

This reminds me of my grandfather, a retired foreman bricklayer, living with us at the time, who resumed work at the camp described as '... the easiest job I ever had...'. He supervised the semi-skilled workmen who could lay bricks in a straight line, but who called him when they reached a corner, window or door. He would then lay the next few bricks to set them on their way again and go back, I imagine, to his cosy hut and tea and a pipe!

The old Hitchin electricity works built by the Electrical Supply Corporation Limited of London in about 1906, stood behind Mr Masters' yard and can still be seen now refurbished and incorporated into William Ransom's research laboratories. Tony Foster recounts its history in *Market Town*.

Moving on, past more allotments the four pretty cottages pictured in several old Hitchin publications have long gone but the two semi-detached houses and the entrance to Ransom's, still remain as does the picturesque little building on the other side of the entrance used as a shoe repairer's for many years right up to the present day.'

Whinbush Grove

The road has always been unadopted. Jeeves the builder built numbers 1 - 8 between 1856, when he became tenant of the land, and 1878 when, as owner, he conveyed some of the

The thatched cottages (above) stood on the west side of the road and were demolished in 1963, left.

southern part to John Hall.

Whinbush House was most probably the first to be built (the houses were erected in two lots of four) and it is very likely that No. 8 was built in 1868. In 1852 the only building on this parcel of land was a large shed, which Jeeves' daughter, Miss Ada Jeeves, came to use for her pony and trap and which still exists. She had a right of way into Whinbush Road.

Behind the houses in Whinbush Grove, their right of way included access to a pump house. It is said that the land at the top (No. 11) was an orchard of which one pear tree remains today.

The Grove was a large Victorian house close by, which became a school, The Sacred Heart Convent, run by French nuns and which has since been demolished.

WALSWORTH ROAD

Walsworth Road appears on the 1818 Plan of the Town and Parish of Hitchin as simply a road to Baldock. At this time, of course, there was no town of consequence inbetween. It is generally agreed that Walsworth means 'Farm of the serfs or Britons'. Ekwall describes it as 'worth of the Welshman or Welshmen'. Worth means 'homestead'.

In the seventeenth century it seems the Walsworth hamlet was brought to book for not repairing the causey (or causeway – a raised footpath) over the Common, as it was a route to the church and market. At times it seems Walsworth Road itself has been impassable and complaints were being made as late as the 1880's. The road, as it is now, is about half a mile long and with the now Cambridge Road, was important enough as a highway for the bridge over the Purwell to be constructed in the 1830's, repaired in the 1880's and widened in 1913.

In 1844 Walsworth Road was still called the Baldock Road. However, maps held at Hitchin Museum, dated 1851 and 1886 show the change to Walsworth Road had taken place. George Beaver calls it 'the Walsworth Road' in 1855 but by the 1880s it was also known as Station Road because of the coming of the railway. Temporarily building plots fronting the road, reached unprecedented heights.

Occasionally one still encounters very elderly people who refer to Walsworth Road as 'Station Road'. Over the last century the two names seem to have been concurrent. The coming of the railway in 1850 must have created a need to differentiate between Walsworth Road and the then track called Nightingale Road, because both roads led to Walsworth. Indeed, as the new buildings linking the town with the station were built from the 1860's and commuting started to be a way of life for some, the name 'Station Road' implied progress and suggested a closeness to the modern artery of communication.

It became fashionable to live in this area and Jeeves the builder no doubt had many satisfied customers, judging by the size and quality of the houses built. These were not artisans' dwellings like those in Nightingale or Radcliffe Roads, these were town houses for people with servants and status. A few had stabling facilities, set in their own private plot behind walls, railings and hedges. The professional classes were ideally suited halfway between town and station, with schools and the socially accepted St Saviour's Church, (a foundation which had sprung fresh from the ideals of the Oxford Movement) on their doorsteps.

The Reverend Gainsford himself lived in a large house along the road on a plot still known as 'Woodside'. The present car park still houses the remains of the stable block of this residence. As the rooks and crows gathered in the trees above this pleasant area an elderly resident in the 1960's used to look up and say 'The Gainsford scholars are going to their rest'.

The road had industry and commerce at one end, Anglican and Baptist churches in the middle and a select tree-lined avenue leading to the newly constructed Hermitage Road (1875). The road quickly became a very busy thoroughfare. Mr Seebohm even built himself an 'underpass' from his Hermitage Gardens (at the rear of Hermitage Road shops, Ransom's side) to his private woodland in Rawling's Dell, presently the sadly neglected Woodside Open Air Theatre.

At the station end stood Bowman's flour mill, a steam mill complete with chimney. This was built in 1901 and stayed until 1986 having outgrown the limitations of the site. The firm, which had started at Astwick before the turn of the century, also traded at Ickleford Mill, as indeed they still do. The firm B & Q developed the site after Bowman's closed.

Mrs Nellie Coxall, (née Charles) remembers that the Bowmans were 'gentlemen'. She was

Left and below: No.110, built by Frederick Jeeves for his family in the 1880s. He stands in the doorway. His daughter, Lizzie Jeeves lived there until 1953.

Below: An uncluttered Walsworth Road, looking towards the station.

there in the office during the First World War. She used to do the accounts and all the book-keeping and took a real pride in all the bills she sent out. One Friday she had done all her bills and had gone home for the weekend. When she got in on the Monday morning mice had eaten all the paperwork! Every Tuesday Mr Harold Bowman would leave an instruction for his bag to be packed and then he would go off to the Corn Exchange. If Mrs Coxall had forgotten anything he would telephone from the town and ask her to bring it up to him. Use of the phone had a hidden hazard. Her predecessor had died of tuberculosis and so as each call had to be made, Nellie had to disinfect the mouthpiece!

Next to Bowman's was a tiny cottage surrounded by a hedge where the Carrington family of tailors had lived in the nineteenth century. Adjacent to this was Mrs Rosamund's tobacconist shop with barbers at the rear; just the place to smarten up after a long day on the Great Northern Railway. Then came a factory which dominated the scene for over half-a-century, the firm of Geo. W King.

G H Innes & Co. & Geo. W King Ltd

Originating in the Market Place, the agricultural engineering firm of G H Innes, whose grass rollers and harrows can still occasionally be seen lying in local farmyards, moved to Walsworth Road at the turn of the twentieth century. During World War One an American, originally called Henry Mayer who later wished to be known as George Walter King, had taken over the firm which subsequently became Innes, Sons & King. He increased its production of agricultural implements and widened the range to include high class dairy equipment.

Each one of his children had the name 'Mayer' incorporated in their Christian names. His youngest son, Hartford Mayer King, was named after the ancestral home in Hartford, Connecticut. One of the sons, Harry, ran the firm with his father and it eventually became known as Geo W King and the address became 'Hartford Works'; a relic of this can be seen as the name still exists on an electricity sub-

station adjacent to the site.

Production later expanded to specialise in conveyors and sliding doors, heavy lifting gear and mechanical handling machinery of all kinds. In 1952, after the site had become too cramped, the firm moved to its other factory in Stevenage. Eventually the firm became a subsidiary of Camford Engineering. The Walsworth Road site became a branch of Staples Matresses and later underwent demolition as new factory units took its place.

Craftsmen of all sorts set up in the road, the raw materials of their trade arriving via the Great Northern or Midland Railway Companies. Builders, plumbers, glaziers, carpenters and even a firm of ceremonial banner makers, Herbert Sharp, have flourished between Verulam Road and the station. A stone masons, Peppers, has existed for most of the century.

Ralph E Sanders

One firm which needed a wide variety of craft skills had its roots in the horse age. Ralph E Sanders was established in Royston in the 1870's. They were coachbuilders who later produced a car called the 'Rational'. Buying out the firm of Odell in Bridge Street in 1900, the carriage construction industry expanded just at a time when motor body building was a prosperous avenue to pursue. Incidentally, the words 'Odell's Carriage Repository' could still faintly be seen above their former premises in Bridge Street until the 1980's.

Sanders had a carriage and motor works purpose-built in Walsworth Road in 1906. Part of these premises still stand, in use today as a tyre and exhaust centre. Originally in a much larger building, motor engineering took place on the ground floor while bodies were built in the loft above. All bodies were wheeled down a brick ramp to the street below, no cumbersome block and tackle haulage here! While Sanders did not make vehicles on the Hitchin site, they fitted bodies to high-class proprietary chassis and sold them as a completed unit. The late Mr Fred Weston, who had been a chauffeur for Mr Purvis of Chiltern Road, remembered being told that if he would collect a car from Sanders

Top: Munitions work - making 1311 shells at Innes and King's factory in 1914. Mr 'Bert' Wells was soon to leave for France.
Above: Gulley grating from this factory still in use in the town centre.
Right: Advertisement in 1915 Almanack and Directory.

WALSWORTH ROAD HITCHIN

Above: Tranquility in Walsworth Road, looking towards the town centre in 1912. The Wall on the left was mainly constructed of clinker from local ironfounders.

A high-class French chassis united with a Sanders body in 1908. The car is a Cottin et Desgouttes. This photograph was taken across the road from the motorworks. Most advertising pictures were taken from this side of the road, with the large house and railings in the background.

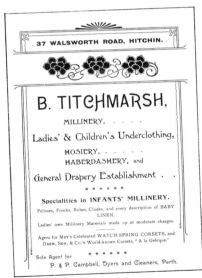

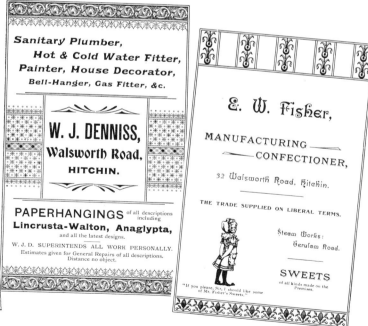

Top: *Church Parades were a feature of life in this area. On this march (26th July 1913) Church stalwarts protested against Government proposals to sever links between the Anglican Church and the State in Wales.*

Above: *Advertisements from the 1890s, to be found in local directories.*

and drive it through Hitchin market on market day, that would be sufficient test of his driving skill to warrant being given the job! This was in the early 1920's.

During the period immediately following the Hitchin Pageant of 1951 'Kershaw's Hitchin Coach' could be seen behind an upper window in Sanders' works. Their former products still turn up for sale at the Reading Carriage Sales and a beautiful pony trap of their manufacture can be seen in the London Science Museum, the name visible on a brass plate inside the rear entrance door.

Thomas Brooker & Sons

Another well-known name in the town, Thomas Brooker & Sons once had two premises along this road. This family firm, dating back to 1876, had a general ironmongery business to the town centre side of the Albert pub and a furniture emporium to the station-side of Dacre Road. Mr Jarman, in the 1950s, would dispense string, clothes pegs, chicken wire, nails and paraffin from a wonderful building. All purchases went into the once familiar Brookers' brown-paper-with-blue-writing packages. The smells from that shop, soap, candles, floor polish and creosote are totally absent from the modern Bucklersbury shop. Mr B W G Ford remembers:

'Having lost our family business and home in the London Blitz of 1940 we came to Stevenage, my paternal grandmother's birthplace, as refugees or 'roughugees' to the locals. I went to work at Brookers as a junior clerk with all the associated jobs including nipping in to the 'Cabin' next door for the chelsea buns etcetera. for the office tea breaks; handwriting the estimates and repair bills for the maintenance work carried out by Mr Parcell and others on various HUDC and HRDC properties as instructed by Mr Harold Brooker (great uncle of the present generation in Bucklersbury). The office was run by Mr Tom Baldry (of Hitchin Youth Club fame in later years) and staffed by Mr Holloway (frequently clad in plus-four suits), Mr Blows from Stevenage and a lady Miss ... (whose name eludes me). The shop downstairs being in the capable hands of Mr Jarman, a Mr Taylor and like myself a teenager Mr Dennis Hagger. The associated furniture shop across Dacre Road was run by Mr Gibbs. I also remember commuting, or whatever it was called fifty years ago, on a £3-19s-0d Hercules bicycle to and from Stevenage and Walsworth Road each day, including a return trip in our one-and-a-quarter hour lunch break, but, of course, I was, or must have been, a lot fitter in those days.'

Travellers to Hitchin were spoilt for choice for refreshment and lodgings. There was the impressive Railway Inn, later the Station Hotel, with important stabling facilities at the rear beyond a carriage arch. It was a Lucas Brewery House and later became a Flowers House. In the 1960's it was renamed 'The Talisman', after a long distance express train of the time, the seats outside also had name boards reminiscent of locomotive name plates. Its last name was Jeans, an attempt to make it an up-market place of entertainment for young drinkers. For many years folk singers had made it a popular venue. It succumbed to the demolisher's hammer in the 1980's after standing forlorn and part burnt-out for some years. A handsome brick office complex now occupies the site.

Further along came the Albert pub, fortunately still with us. It was built around the time the railway was being constructed and the landlord, Mr Estwick, obliged his customers by opening very early in the morning. No doubt this is how it became known as 'The Early Bird'. In June 1869 the Hertfordshire Express reported that a runaway horse had knocked down a lamp-post outside The Early Bird pub. That same year Mr Estwick applied for a spirit licence but a petition of one hundred people headed by the Reverend George Gainsford said there were five other houses where brandy could be obtained. In support of the application Mr Times gave evidence that he had suffered an accident outside the house and had received '... great kindness from Mr and Mrs Estwick and a glass of brandy would have been most welcome'. The application was turned down! In

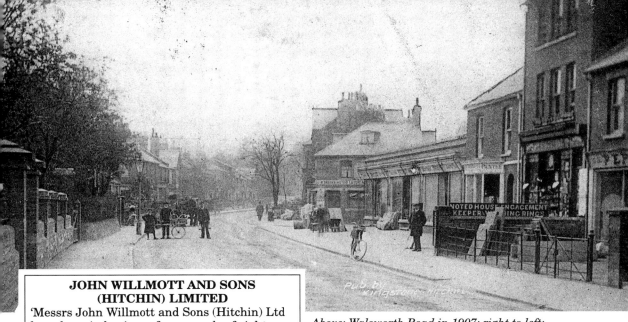

JOHN WILLMOTT AND SONS (HITCHIN) LIMITED

'Messrs John Willmott and Sons (Hitchin) Ltd have been in business for upwards of eighty years and have carried on a general Building & Contracting business in Hitchin for over fifty years. During this time they have carried out works of every description in most parts of England. Locally some of the most important works carried out by them were the Hitchin Girls' Grammar School and recently the Hitchin Boys' Grammar School. The building of the Letchworth Abattoir, St Christopher School, Letchworth and Letchworth Railway Station. They have carried out works for public bodies, including the London County Council, the Air Ministry, the Admiralty, the L and N E Railway Co. and various County Councils. Recently large contracts have been executed in the reconstruction of Aylesbury and Clacton Railway Stations and the building of the Nurses' Home at Barnet for the Barnet Board of Guardians.'

1931 Hitchin Official Guide

Above: Walsworth Road in 1907: right to left: Pepper's stonemasons, next, what became Samm's Chemists, then Denniss's decorators business, then Brooker's furniture shop.
Below: Unique in Hitchin: fine Victorian chimney pots on No.110.

1873 for a short time, the pub was re-named the Prince Albert but later became known as just The Albert.

Opposite this, on a Jeeves-built corner site stood a Temperance hotel for the use of cyclists. Curiously enough, cyclists still flock here because the family firm of C J Frost, established in the town for nearly half-a-century, trades in everything for the pedal-powered.

Next to The Albert, past Brookers shop, stood the Acacia Hotel. In later years this became the Acacia Cafe. Mr Matthews from Baldock remembers that there was a grisly murder here in the 1920s. The culprit, who had the memorable name of Eugene De Vere, was apprehended by Detective Rogers after a tip off. This is a far cry from the romantic origin of the building now occupied by Mary Collins. The property, entirely constructed of concrete, is believed to have been a wedding present from a London judge to his daughter. If the construction methods were revolutionary, the provision of carriage and stabling facilities must have made it a very attractive proposition, especially since it had maids' accommodation in a wooden pitched roof, which unfortunately is no longer there, having burnt down years ago.

The Radcliffe Arms was once called The Rugeley Arms. In 1856 it became The Nightingale but by 1869 it had assumed its present identity. William Richardson, the publican at this time, was fined twenty shillings for selling porter before the legal time on a Sunday morning. The Radcliffe Arms has an attractive sign board with the arms of the Radcliffe family.

There is no longer a pharmacist along Walsworth Road. Until the 1960's, for as long as anyone could remember, there was a chemist and photographic suppliers in the road. His name was G W Samm and his qualification diploma, which hung proudly in his shop, was dated 1913. Local legend had it that he had been a medical orderly in World War One and knew more about curing ailments than the average doctor. He certainly engendered an air of mystery in the childish mind. On entering the empty shop one would wait until this tall, aged alchemist-like figure descended through the bead curtains from the back room. The thin veil concealed all sorts of mysteries for those with a vivid imagination. He moved silently with few words. His prescriptions came in cardboard pill boxes and coloured bottles, not in proprietary plastic hygienery! On Sunday evenings he could be seen taking the air on a short stroll between his shop and a house in Trevor Road, always accompanied by two elderly ladies, one on each arm. He appeared to be politely listening as they discussed and argued the topics of the day with him.

A building which started life as an iron structure, Walsworth Road Baptist Church, was inspired by Richard Johnson, the Chief Engineer of the Great Northern Railway. He had it built in 1867 to serve the new railway community and within a few years it was to be replaced by the brick structure we know today. Next to this thriving church stood a building which has only recently been demolished, the Hitchin Youth Centre. In addition to Aillie Latchmore's Clubland for girls in St John's Road, a youth club was constructed on a site which is now developed as a red brick housing complex, Harrison Close. A temporary wooden structure which was later extended held a successful youth club from the end of World War Two until the 1970's. The annual pantomime which the Youth Centre produced at the Town Hall was a regular mecca for all local children in the post-Christmas period. Many gifted sportsmen and women played in teams associated with the Youth Centre. The leader for most of the Centre's existence was Mr Tom Baldry who lived in the house next door.

When one walks along this road to town one must look at the faded opulence of the houses between Verulam Road and Whinbush Road. These buildings had spacious grounds with walled gardens, servants' quarters and a warm elegance which only brick can give. The chimneys and roof tiles of this road speak volumes about the range of products available to the Victorian builder. A tradition which was often carried out in the past was that of the 'topping out' ceremony. When a building was finished the names of the workers, a newspaper or coin of the day, were placed in a bottle and put under the end ridge tile. If one looks carefully one can see a bottle in just such a position on the roof of the cottage which links Walsworth Road with Whinbush Road. This attractive cottage, which has been much photographed in the past, was originally thatched but this particular roofing material disappeared many years ago.

In a road where culture and benevolence were features of the nineteenth century life, culture and art still flourish and it is fitting that they continue on land once owned by the Gainsfords. The Queen Mother Theatre and Woodside Hall, the new buildings erected for the Thespians' use continue to enrich our lives towards the end of the twentieth century. Reverend George Bernard Gainsford himself was keen to support amateur theatrical and operatic performances. He would surely be proud to see his land being put to such use.

Above: 1936 Advertisement in the Hitchin Guide.
Right: Demolition of Bowman's Mill in 1986.
Below: The mill flourished on this site from 1901,
and after demolition trade continued and expanded
at Ickleford.

RADCLIFFE ROAD

When Radcliffe Road was built, immediately after the railway had reached Hitchin, a curate at St Mary's, George Gainsford, had already seen the need for a spiritual centre in the area. He left Hitchin in 1854 but when he returned he financed the building of St Saviour's Church and became its first priest. The Gainsfords, father and son, influenced the sacred as well as the secular life of the community for seventy years. Gainsford Senior saw a school, orphanage and almshouses built opposite his church, all in matching style. A whole community saw practical Christianity in action and most were influenced to some degree by it.

St Saviour's school was opened in 1868. It had lower and upper girls departments and a separate building for infants. At times there were three classes in one room. Older boys were sent either to St Mary's or the British Schools. By the turn of the century the senior mistress was Miss Rainbird who lived in Dacre Road, the infants being looked after by Miss Heeps. The infant department was the private concern of Reverend Gainsford.

Nellie Coxall, (née Charles) remembers:-

'When I look back... Miss Rainbird, have you heard of her? She was a Headmistress and she couldn't have been very old, she used to come in the mornings and say 'Girls ...Girls... my neuralgia ... is terrible, please be quiet!'. There were three classes in one room, years later I took meals-on-wheels to Miss Rainbird and I never told her – I wasn't very popular with her anyway. Every morning we had hymns and before dinner we had grace, went home, had a dinner, Mother was very religious, we had grace again and we had to take it in turns round the table and I had one brother who was very naughty, he was a twin, the other one died, and sometimes he wouldn't say it and we were sitting and my other brother would kick him and then I would kick him, then I would

say to mother 'can I say it?' and she would say 'Yes - now put Harry's dinner outside, Harry can have it when he comes home'... get back to school, another grace. In the afternoon we didn't finish till nearly four, another prayer and 'Now the day is ended' or if we didn't have that we had 'The day thou gavest Lord is ended'. I look back and laugh at it all, really!'

Joan Taylor (née Weston) remembers that Miss Rainbird was friendly with Miss Surridge, Head of Walsworth School in the late 1920s. Staff names included Miss Tompkins who was very 'avant-garde' since she came in from Preston on a motorcycle; Mrs Dowling who was an Anglo-Indian who lived latterly in York Road, Miss Bannister, soon replaced by Miss Baxter and Miss Russell who later became Mrs Hawkins of the family outfitter's business. The school song started:-

'Sunny, straight and steady' is the motto of our school,
Dear children are we ready to keep the golden rule?'

The school functioned until the 1950s and was used on Sundays as the Sunday School which in later years was run by the Sayer family. When the school closed part of the building was used as the Gainsford Memorial Hall for social functions, the old church hall in Garden Row (latterly run as the school canteen) was used by the Bancroft Players under the name St Anne's Hall. The rest of the building was bought by Allam's Wholesale Confectioners and latterly by a Cash & Carry firm. Housing development now stands on the site.

The orphanage was opened in 1873 and was built to house between fifteen and twenty-five girls. By 1899 it was run by the Sisters of St Margaret's, East Grinstead. It had its own chapel for private worship and employed a Matron. In later years the organisation passed

PROGRAMME

THE St. SAVIOUR'S PLAYERS

present

THE GHOST TRAIN

A Drama In Three Acts

by

Arnold Ridley

By arrangement with Samuel French Ltd.

In

St. SAVIOUR'S PARISH HALL

FRIDAY 16th JUNE.   8.15 p.m.

SEAT No.

Top: St Saviour's Sunday School Treat in 1909. Notice the sub-post office to the left of the picture.
Above: The orphanage, St Bridget (taken in 1992) and now converted into flats.
Right The last production of the pre-war period!
Below right: Ecclesiastical footscraper! (Drawn by Becky Hull).

to a new trust and many older residents will remember Sister Elizabeth who lived there. In earlier times the orphans wore blue dresses and pinafores with heavy red-lined cloaks in winter. The later regime dispensed with the uniform and changed the name of the orphanage to St Bridget. John Myatt lived here when it became a private dwelling and ran a printing business from the premises while also working as a music teacher. The matron of the orphanage, Ida Bridges, founded St Saviour's Players which functioned in the old green corrugated St Anne's Hall.

The almshouses, known as 'The Cloisters' were built in 1896 and provided nine dwellings for the elderly of the parish whether male or female, married or single. There was a resident Parish Nurse who lived in the room above the doorway. Mrs Gainsford would apparently always send for her in times of

Reverend Scott presides over a Parish 'welcome home' party in 1946

illness before going to Dr Gilbertson who lived nearby in Walsworth Road.

Although the only commercial premises in the road were Arnsby's Dairy at the bottom right-hand side and the Walsworth Road sub-post office on the top corner, shops were always close at hand in other adjacent roads. When Mrs C F Alexander wrote, 'The rich man in his castle, The poor man at his gate', she envisaged a Victorian pecking order. As one looks down the road from Walsworth Road the houses seem to rise the nearer one gets to the church, with the most attractive middle-class houses, with potential for servants, closest to the church. In Victorian times St Saviour's was the 'Society Church'. The modern developers have removed some of the sub-standard artisans' dwellings and replaced them with buildings in scale with the rest of the properties. The red brick harmonises subtly with the older structures. Religious harmony exists too since Gainsford's school is now a Sikh Temple.

BENSLOW LANE

The name Benslow may possibly be derived from 'Benchelowe Pece', an ancient field name. The Tithe map of 1818 shows several pieces of land in the area: Great Benslow Hills, Little Benslow Hills, Benslow Hill Shot. In 1851, we find Benslow Lane being called Benchley Hills Road. In 1869 it was still a country lane, though Benslow Terrace (numbers 21 and 29) was 'in situ' by 1864.

By 1900 most of the street had been developed. The lane had been widened to provide adequate access for the new houses in the street.

In the early years of the century cows were regularly herded down Benslow Lane to be milked and then taken back to graze on the fields at the top of the road.

They belonged to Wallace Dairies in Bancroft and keen gardeners would rush out to sweep up the manure. A boy with a broom swept up the rest. Now Benslow Lane is full of traffic, with parking for residents and commuters as well as people calling at St Andrew's School, Pinehill Hospital and Little Benslow Hills music school.

There are also a large number of homes that did not exist earlier this century, when Benslow Lane was in the country and families would come up on a Sunday afternoon to picnic.

When the walkers reached halfway up the lane, to just below where St Andrew's School stands now, the trees would arch overhead and they would pass through a tunnel of leaves, overhanging a high boarded fence on either side of the lane.

The Co-op regularly held its fête on the fields where Benslow Rise stands now and Sunday schools held outings there. Although the bottom of Benslow Lane was full of houses built in the 1860s and '70s, there were very few homes at the top – but they were grand ones.

Businessman William Ransom, the founder of the distillery firm, built a house called Fairfield which in later years was owned by members of the Seebohm family. They left it to the Rural School of Music. The site of St Andrew's School was also donated by Miss Esther Seebohm when she died.

William's brother, Alfred Ransom, lived nearby in another large house, now Benslow Nursing Home. It was the first site of Girton College and six young ladies arrived to study in 1869, much to the indignation of many locals who thought universities for women were a waste of time. The young ladies were considered very 'stuck up' - they didn't say 'hello' and walked with their noses in the air. After four years Girton College moved to Cambridge. Alfred Ransom's house was later bought by builder Matthew Foster, father of the historian Tony. Later still it became a maternity home, run by Mrs Dawes, and then a nursing home run by John Powers. Its lodge (Banksia Lodge) is in Benslow Lane but the Nursing Home entrance is in Benslow Rise. It is now surrounded by houses built soon after the Second World War by the Foster family.

Mrs Edna Taylor remembers living at Banksia Lodge around the time of the First World War.

'Course there were lime kilns at the bottom...we called it the 'chute', it was quite dangerous there, you see they (the workmen) used to come in down where my grandparents cottage was, that side, the workmen to the lime kilns, and they had big round chimneys and ...oh...it was white as could be down there...they looked almost like something from outer space when you looked down and saw these huge buildings, I never went down there...well couldn't get down....but that brings me to Belladonna...whether it was the birds or what but we could find it at the top there, seeds had been scattered down. From Banksia Lodge there was a tunnel...well it came from the lime kilns into my father's garden...I don't

Seen outside Benslow House in 1918 are (L to R) Ernest Cotton, Mr Cooper (owner), Elizabeth Cotton, Mrs Cooper, with dog Winkie, Edna Cotton and Kate Cotton.

remember it being used...it looked so dark....if you stood on the chute you knew just where it was, ...it was where they cut away all the chalk and of course after they cut it away, then the rains came and it started slipping...we always said 'down the chute' or 'be careful of the chute' we knew what we was talking about...there was no fence there as well, there was no point because it would slide you know, like the Norfolk coast, giving away...!'

From about 1920 there were one and then two nurseries at the top of Benslow Lane leading to the bridge over the railway. The first bridge, too low for electric trains, was wider than the present one and was used by lorries and cars, although it was only built for farm carts. It was the only single span bridge for miles around and was blown up by British Rail at two am on Sunday July 28 1974. The blast cracked panes of glass nearby.

The German Hospital, now Pinehill, was built in Benslow Lane in 1908 as a convalescent home for the German community in England. Hitchin was chosen for its fresh country air and the foundation stone was laid by Princess Louise Augusta of Schleswig-Holstein. Later it was used for old people and TB patients, and is now a private hospital.

On the opposite side of Benslow Lane were two kilns and a lime quarry, which was excavated by hand until it was exhausted, in about 1928 or '29. The quarrying was started by Alfred Ransom, William's lesser-known brother. The 1881 Census indicates that he followed a multiplicity of occupations employing many people. As a farmer Alfred owned and worked three hundred and seventy acres, employing twenty-seven men and nine boys; as a brick-maker he employed seven men and two boys; and as a lime burner he employed as many as thirty-four men and three boys, even though this was not a pleasant occupation.

The 1915 Directory shows that his son, Theodore, had taken over the brick-making business in Bethel Lane (now St John's Road).

Quarrying moved over to the other side of the railway line and the workers finally got a steam shovel to ease their load.

A fence was finally put up alongside Benslow Lane to protect people from the sheer one hundred foot drop towards the railway line. Within a few years silver birch trees grew up in the sparse soil but they were later cut down to build workshops.

St Andrew's School was the last building to be put up in the middle section of the lane, erected in 1969 on land left by Miss Seebohm. This was the long-awaited successor to the school in Hollow Lane, bringing pupils back to the area once served by St Saviour's School. Pupils from St Mary's School moved here, with their Head, Bob Price, at this time. St Mary's was then demolished.

HIGHBURY ROAD

The 1881 Ordnance Survey map of Hitchin shows the road to Highbury strongly marked on the map, but as yet unnamed. Running from Walsworth Road, by the side of the newly-erected Baptist Chapel and Sunday School (1867), it is bordered by fields and contains only two large houses. On the right stands Hillside, built in 1866 for Richard Johnson, Chief Engineer to the Great Northern Railway. Higher up, on the left, we find the large red-brick Highbury House, (1874) with coach house and extensive grounds.

> 'Southward . . . is Highbury, partly laid out as a building estate which, from its elevated site, is rapidly being occupied by good private residences . . .'
> *(Extract from the 1899 Handbook Hitchin and the Neighbourhood).*

By 1890, George Beaver, Hitchin's Surveyor, speaks of widening the 'Highbury' Road. The map of 1898 shows considerable change. Not only was the road now named, but the former large field to the east, had fallen prey to the developers, as Hitchin continued to expand. Building plots were determined by the existing field-boundaries and footpaths. Seven substantially-built houses now fronted the road, with plots awaiting others. Opposite however, the scene remained unchanged, still rural, bordered by trees, with allotment gardens at the Hollow Lane end of the hill.

Highbury itself was an area where several small roads and lanes converged, separating plots of cultivated land, interspersed with a few small cottages.

The year 1897 saw the first row of terraced houses being built at the Whitehill Road junction, aptly named 'Diamond Jubilee Terrace'. These were shortly followed by a similar row on the opposite side of the road (the New Century Cottages of 1901). By the beginning of the First World War increased housing development resulted in the area being divided for administrative convenience into Highbury, Highbury (White Hill), Highbury Road, Highbury (Devonshire View), Highbury (Providence Terrace, Bethel Lane) and Highbury (Riddy View)!

Life in this new suburb was not without incident:-

> 'The Surveyor reported that on the night of the 22nd or 23rd the new seat in the Highbury Road was wilfully broken from its fastenings and thrown into the road. It was resolved to offer a reward of £1.00 for information leading to the conviction of the offender or offenders'.
> *(Hitchin Urban District Council Minutes 23rd September 1903)*

Caldicott House - Highbury Road

'Bounded on the East side by Highbury Road, on the South by a Private Road to the prettily Wooded Plantation Shrubbery, Dell and Rookery belonging to F Seebohm Esq., West by the Pleasure Grounds of 'Woodside' belonging to the Rev G Gainsford, on the North by Lot 2 and the Trustees of the Walsworth Road Baptist Church'.

This was the description by Jackson's Auctioneers for the sale of 'Brockton House' (later Caldicott House) on '...Tuesday March 31st 1903 at 5 o'clock prompt'. It failed to reach its reserve price of £3,400 but was later sold to J Heald Jenkins for £3,200 for a 'prep' school for The Leys, Cambridge and Mill Hill. The auctioneer had called the '...especial attention of City Gentlemen to this property, it being reached within five minutes walk of the station from whence Kings Cross is reached in about forty two minutes... Erected in 1866 regardless of expense in Gothic Style...'.

A rough sketch of land at that time

The land was originally owned by William Wilshere who died in 1824. It passed through various hands and the house named 'Hillside' was thought to have been built by Richard Johnson. He had been appointed Chief Engineer of the Great Northern Railway in 1861. In 1882 'Hillside' was sold to Joseph Bettinson who renamed the house 'Brockton House' after his grandmother, Ann Brockton. It remained with the Bettinsons until its sale in 1903.

Caldicott School.

James Heald Jenkins, the first headmaster, was the son of a President of the Methodist Conference. He attended the Leys School and later returned as a master. The foundation of the Leys School was rooted in Methodism. Mr Jenkins married Theodora Caldicott Ingram and Brockton House was renamed Caldicott School after her. The school began in January 1904 with eight boys and by 1908 there were

Highbury post office and the New Century Cottages built in 1901. The original pillar box is still 'in situ'.

thirty-nine boys. It had no direct connection with Hitchin except an association with Brand Street Methodist Chapel.

A great deal of alteration and extension took place between 1904 and 1915. Mr Jenkins bought the Lodge and gardens from Richard Johnson and the Baptist Trustees for £800. A gymnasium and a chapel were built. Gordon Wood joined the staff in 1912 and later became Headmaster in 1927. Miss Margaret Ingram ('Inky') joined the staff in 1913. With two other mistresses she carried the burden of teaching during the 1914-1918 war. The main playing field was on the London Road. Each Monday the pupils walked in crocodile to Hitchin town swimming baths in Queen Street. These baths were emptied every Sunday, and refilled from the River Hiz. The boys did 'physical jerks' at 7.45 am in an outdoor compound called the 'Henna' (Gehenna?).

Towards the end of the war Hitchin was bombed by a Zeppelin near the railway. All the boys were in bed when a huge rattling noise developed like several express trains, then some loud bangs and the ground shook. The boys were comforted with apples and biscuits in the dining room and taken the next day to

see the craters. In 1919 the War Memorial Gate (still on the Walsworth Road) was dedicated to thirteen pupils who had died.

Many fond memories have been recorded by old pupils of these early days, but conditions were spartan. The boys washed in enamel bowls sometimes having to break the ice. In the grim winter of 1917 even the gas meter froze! Punishment by cane in a private section of the house was usually followed by a piece of cake to show no hard feelings.The question of food values had the special attention of medical advisers and there was a liberal allowance of fresh fruit, vegetables, eggs and milk throughout the year. The Scout movement was very strong and a Christian atmosphere prevailed. The caretaker/gardener's son recalls the wild birds, (over forty different species were recorded) the beautiful surroundings and the delightful atmosphere

Eventually the school needed larger premises. In 1938 F Gordon Wood surrendered the lease and the school moved to Farnham

These 'Gentlemen's Residences' were built by Jeeves with the early commuter in mind (postcard dated 1910).

Royal, Slough. It still retains its name, The Caldicott School. The organ from the chapel on the Hitchin site, dedicated in 1932, was moved with the school and is still in use.

From 1939-1944 the property was taken over by the War Office. Regiments were sometimes stationed there before going overseas. In 1944 - 1945 Mr Jenkins sold the property and, due to the generosity of Colonel J F Harrison of Kings Walden, it became available to Hitchin Youth Centre Association latterly known as Hitchin Youth Trust. In 1950 it was leased to the Ministry of Works. Many people remember taking their driving test from there!

Part of the land was sold for redevelopment in 1984. At that time the 'new' Youth Club building was pulled down. A new charitable company was formed, The Caldicott Centre Ltd which provides youth clubs and activities for young people under twenty-five. They are based in the house.

The outbuildings have been used for other youth organisations, boxing is held in the gym and weight lifting in the chapel. Scouts and Guides use the old school library and reading room.

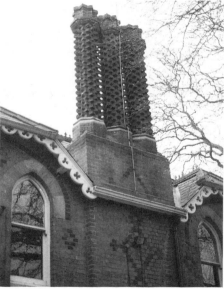

Top: Main house of Caldicott School.
Above left: School open day photographed by Latchmore in 1913.
Above: Ornate chimneys on Caldicott House.
Left: Page from HUDC Official Guide 1910.

Gargoyles, Gables and Finials

Prior to the introduction of industrialised methods, these forms of ornamentation were often carved by hand in stone or wood. The Victorians found terracotta to be cheaper, manufactured with the help of machinery.

Most ornamentation took the form of six main themes, those being geometric shapes, abstract lines, vegetation, animals, mythical creatures and human scenes. In Hitchin there are examples of both Gothic functional forms (the gargoyles of St Mary's Church and the ridge tile finials of Brotherhood House) and later non-functional decoration (the dragon finial in Whitehill Road).

The rows and rows of Victorian terraced houses were given some degree of individuality with decorative roof tiles topped with finials of different designs for each house. The simplest being used for low-budget houses, while more affluent detached properties would carry the most elaborate designs of grotesque dragons and gargoyles. This form of decoration made for a most interesting skyline from which one could see at a glance the status and income of the residents!

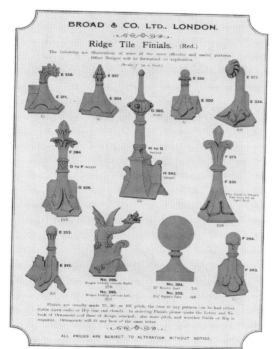

Above: Terracotta dragon finial gracing the roof of 31 Whitehill Road. The unusual floral form can be seen in West Hill.

Above: Many of these finials can be spotted on Hitchin rooftops (catalogue 1910).
Right: Ridge tiles and finials from Verulam Road.

THE AVENUE

The Nettledell Fields for a time gave their name to the developments around The Avenue and Highbury which were, during building, described as the Nettledell Estate. We have George Beaver's splendid diary entry for 1894. He hired a pony and trap and went to:-

'....the new road works being done in the Nettledell Field....I drive into the road from the Walsworth Road and out again into the Great Wymondley Road thereby practically opening the road altho' in an unfinished state'. He goes on to say 'My first surveys of these fields....with a view to ultimate building purposes was made in the years 1863-4'. The new road he refers to is most probably The Avenue and the first house went up in 1896 (No. 3). The trees in the road were planted especially for the street, hence 'The Avenue'.

Right: Wilton Lodge, built and occupied by the French family in 1896, was the first house in the road (note the scaffolding). 'Red Gables' stands on the right.
Below: Early view, post-marked 1916. 'Otterburn' (1930) is on the right.

Above left and right: Fine examples of individuality to be found in the road. Note the warm terracotta tiling and the unusual carved window supports.
Below left: Cast-iron footscraper still 'in situ'.
Below right: Market gardener Fred Cotton's horse, Daisy, waiting at the junction with Chiltern Road (1930s).

CHILTERN ROAD

This last portion of the Nettledell Estate to be developed was released onto the market in 1901. 'Chiltern' comes from the Latin 'Celsus' meaning 'high'. Hitchin is situated in a gap in the Chiltern Hills. Appearances are deceptive, the plots which appear meagre when compared to those in the Avenue, are large by today's standards! The road quickly took on an air of settled respectability. The trees were an early feature, as an extract from the minutes of the Hitchin Urban District Council notes in December 1902. 'Messrs Theodore Ransom, George Wagstaff Russell and Reverend George Bernard Gainsford appointed a Committee to superintend the planting of trees in Chiltern Road by Messrs W Fells & Son'.

Above: Stunning array of Champion Pots!
Below: Postcard dated 1924, looking towards Wymondley Road.

WYMONDLEY ROAD

Wymondley Road has linked Hitchin to Great Wymondley from ancient times. Wymondley is 'Wimundeslai' in the Domesday Book of 1086, ie Wilmund's Leah, leah usually meaning grassland. Great Wymondley's life as a settlement is known to date at least from Roman times. The road known as Wymondley Highway bisected Purwell Field; on the north it sloped to Benslow Hills and Beggarly Shot; to the south was Riddy Shot and Riddy Lane. Field names along the route testify to the village's importance: Wymondley Way Shot, Wymondley Highway, Highway Shot and Wymondley Brook. (A shot is a selion, or cultivated strip in an open field, consisting of a ridge with furrows on either side). However up until the turn of the century it was very much a country lane bounded by the characteristically high banks which marked the end of the strips where the plough was turned. The ridges and furrows at right angles to the highway were clearly visible after the First World War. The land was used by Charles Worbey as market gardens and there were gravel and sand pits. The landscape was dominated by William Ransom's physic fields. Along the Great Wymondley Road were fields of deadly nightshade and of lavender.

In 1901 the country atmosphere was only interrupted by Ransom's house - The Chilterns, with it's extensive outbuildings and greenhouses. Information from Michael Ransom following a conversation with his father Richard Ransom, aged 88 years, about The Chilterns. He recalls that:

'Throughout Hitchin's history the better-off moved to 'new' areas of the town for health reasons. Bancroft provided owners with their own wells in contrast to medieval Back Street. It was because one of his sons contracted tuberculosis that Francis Ransom moved from Bancroft to The Chilterns, Great Wymondley Road, at the turn of the century. Here the elevated position provided fresh air. Richard Ransom was born in the house and much to his chagrin was moved into an attic room at the age of seven years to make way for the last new Ransom baby.

In 1913 Francis Ransom engaged his sister Priscilla's husband, Geoffrey Lucas, as the architect to double the size of the house which included a billiard room. In the garden Mr Ransom grew spectacular rhododendrons, while the greenhouses and fernery were a source of pleasure.

The Ransom's neighbours were George Passingham and George Spurr. The latter lost all his sons in the Great War; his daughter married Mr Crabb, the tailor.

The house was sold to Dr Skeggs towards the end of the First World War and the Ransoms moved to Newlands'. Richard Ransom was grandson to William Ransom, founder of the pharmaceutical firm.

There inevitably followed the development of large 'bijou' residences as the town's élite once more moved to a new sector of Hitchin. Over the next ten years other large houses were built, Connaught House now numbers 23 and 25 (c.1903), Wayshott now number 35 (1904 designed by F W Kinneir Tarte for F P Flint), Dowlands (1904 by Walter Millard for George Spurr), Lavender Croft now number 61 (1910 by Fred Rowntree for Mrs Blackhouse as a Quaker Missionary Children's Home), and Riddy Shott (1907 by Geoffrey Lucas for W O Times).

Riddy Shott

William Onslow Times, 'Mr Hitchin', had several houses built which he subsequently rented out. Riddy Shott was one of them. The late survival of the strip system of land tenure in Hitchin meant the site was accumulated over several years as the necessary small parcels were acquired. Designed by Geoffrey Lucas, it is in the Vernacular Revival style. It was first occupied by two ladies with East

India Company connections who introduced several exotic varieties of plant which still flourish in the garden. From 1917 until 1929 Reginald Hine lived in Riddy Shott and it was in the top floor study that his two volume History of Hitchin (1927, 1929) was written. In 1918 he built on the loggia or garden room, fittingly for an antiquarian it has roof timbers from Hatfield's old vicarage and a Tudor-style door from Horsham jail!

In 1929 the house was auctioned by John Shilcock at the Sun Hotel. Although it was put up as house with separate lot for building land, the whole site was bought by Mr Roberts. He had been wounded in the First World War and the south facing land was ideal for his planned apple orchard. Cox's Orange Pippins from the Riddy Shott orchard were a prized fruit at Covent Garden. Mrs Roberts still lives in the house she had built in the fifties, next door to Riddy Shott; her garden still runs down to Riddy Lane, now a footpath. Eric Dyer, well-known Hitchin butcher and horticulturist bought Riddy Shott. Much of the land was subsequently sold for the development of The Aspens. The apple sheds, 'they were a wonderful store, all insulated with cork', finally disappeared in 1981 when number 54 Wymondley Road was built. Riddy Shott is currently occupied by Dr Gerry Tidy, a local medical practitioner.

Connaught House

The upper stretch of the road developed slowly in the 1920's. The changing face of the road is illustrated by the history of the parcel of land between Connaught House (23/25) and Wayshott (No. 35). Deeds reveal that the land was passed in 1854 from Kemp's Charity, the Trustees of which were a long list of local worthies, to the Delmé-Radcliffe family. Subsequently it became the property of William Onslow Times and John James Shilcock.

Below Chiltern Road, it was still a narrow country lane where two cars could not easily pass. Mrs Ivy Sainsbury (née Pettengell) remembers the road 'a fairly narrow road really because there were no paths....it wasn't

tarmacked, it was a gravelly road, but it was nice and clean generally, I mean it was good enough to run a top along... they would come for Sunday walks, people did in those days'. She also remembers the large hawthorn hedges. In 1933, 'The Chilterns' was demolished and Hitchin welcomed the 1930's with the development of a small estate bearing the same name. White walls and green roofs were a suburban step for the country lane. Ivy Sainsbury remembers that everybody thought them 'new fangled'. They were built by John Ray, the builders. The green roof tiles were ordered from Poole in Dorset. It has remained a fine example of domestic architecture which compliments the Edwardian vernacular and Old English style of the first houses to step out of town. The 1930's also saw the development of well-built detached houses with good-sized gardens along the road and the start of Sorrel Garth. The land ownership moved away from the narrow strips although the old boundaries of small plots still dominate and the names of the owners still reflected townsmen. It can be seen from the maps how the plots determined the nature of the subsequent development.

Mrs Edna Taylor (née Cotton) has many memories of this area, which bring the past alive. Born in Whinbush Road in 1914, she attended St Saviour's School. During the First World War her mother acted as 'Housekeeper' at Highfield in Benslow Lane. By this time the family had moved to the Lodge 'Banksia Cottage' at the top of Benslow Lane (opposite the entrance to what is now Pinehill Hospital). Her grandparents occupied the other lodge house by the railway station.

'...Then my father and mother, they worked hard and saved and saved because my father wanted a place of his own, so he then found a plot of land that he rather fancied in Wymondley Road and he put a brick where he wanted his bungalow, and the bungalow was built, and we lived in Wymondley Road, near the railway bridge...the bungalow is not there now, its called Halsey Drive.

There was Lavender Croft, market gardening, market gardening until you came to these two cottages. Farmers Wallace and

*Left: Architect's drawing of
'Riddy Shott', (1907).
Above: Plaque on the wall of
'Riddy Shott'.*

*Right: Early photograph (1905) of Connaught
House before its division in 1961.
Below: Eddie Edwards tending his beehives at
Connaught House assisted by his Aunt Annie
and sister Dorothea.*

Fred Cotton's 'farm'.

Worbey, they did the ground, then you came to Fred Cotton, which was my father's bungalow. We had ducks, chickens, pigs, horses and, of course, they used to call us 'the farm'. It was a happy time, we worked very hard because at the bungalow we had no water, no electricity and no gas, so you can imagine, can't you.....We had an artesian well just outside the back door, we used to pump that. We had a bathroom and the water would flow away because we had a cesspool, but we had no way of filling the bath except by the copper.I got to school on the milk float! You know the one with the churn and the two wheels? Funnily enough it was a Mr Taylor who used to take me and he had a little seat there and if I was ready in time he used to say 'Come on here, get on there' and we used to go jogging off with a pony on the front. He'd finished all his deliveries you see....this churn..it had a tap at the bottom..I can see it now...galvanised and it had got brass pieces on it, he used to turn the tap on for the milk and pour into a milk jug..and have these things that ladle in, I suppose there was a quarter-pint or half-pint, whatever the good lady needed. At the end of his round when he was going back to Wallace's Dairies, then in Bancroft, and so, of course, he would give me a good run up and drop me off at Verulam Road, and all I had to do was walk down to the school. Then I had a bike so we would bike to school....

My father was a nurseryman but he had pigs...we were breeding pigs too...and I often woke up in the night when she was having her pigs and they used to take the little ones away from her because she, well she was in pain, and bring them into the kitchen and I could hear them grunting away. I think we had three sows. When we used to take her to meet her husband we walked her from here to St Ippollits, it was across fields wasn't it? ....she went at a trot didn't she...we all had to trot...having been once she was off....no flies on pigs! We fed our pigs on bran.. well we used to have an old copper outside, we used to stoke it up, of course we used 'chat' potatoes, they didn't sell so we put those in, those were all the small ones, so we put them in the copper and boy they used to smell lovely! Get them in the pail and slosh around the potatoes and then put the dan in - dan - well it was grain - corn grain almost like flour - dark colour, it smelt nice! Bran we used to give to the horses - on a very cold day a hot bran mash but its different altogether the feeding now - that's why stuff doesn't taste the same I'm sure!

We were breeding ducks, hatching chickens so you can understand them thinking it was a farm - but it wasn't a farm to me.

We didn't have electricity until after the Second World War and then I think father was getting on his feet and father thought he'd try and meet the Marketing Board so far...so we got the water laid on and the electricity. Did we feel cold! You see we only had the Aladdin lamps - just didn't believe we were that short distance from Hitchin and we hadn't all these facilities...they had already got them there..Lavender Croft was electric by then and we were in the dark...the dark years of the war didn't make that difference to me until perhaps I was going to the pictures...

See it all closed in for housing, it was all sold for property and in my day I used to bike around and go to Worbey's, when they were picking strawberries in, like, they were fields. My father wanted so many baskets and I used to get them on my bike and bring them, so it was totally different.'

Left: This charming photograph taken in the mid 1920s, shows a view of Wymondley Road looking towards Hitchin. Sandover Close now stands on the site of the cottages. On the left of the picture is Edna Cotton with her friend Doris and dogs Nina and Gyp.

Left: In the garden at 'Riddy Shott', Mr and Mrs Roberts with their donkey, Thomas.
Below: Taken in 1944 in one of the Worbey brothers' fields, now Coleridge Close. (L to R) Marion Farrow, Bob Grimes, Chris Brown, John Worbey, David Farrow and Brenda Royal.

Richard Tristram's Grave

In a field on the outskirts of Hitchin is a grave. On one side is the Stevenage Road and on another is Folly Brook with the Oakfield Estate beyond. Some eccentric people have chosen to be buried out of consecrated ground for various reasons. One explanation of why Richard Tristram chose to do so was because he had witnessed the bones of earlier burials being unceremoniously thrown out when fresh graves were being dug by the sexton!

Richard was the eldest son of Lawrence and Anne Tristram (née Taverner) and his wife was Dorothy, the daughter of James Cocks of London. Richard Tristram, a Hitchin solicitor who died on 16 November 1734 aged 74, is also commemorated with other members of his family by an inscription in St Mary's Church, Hitchin.

In 1768 his son, Richard, vested the field in trustees so that his father's remains 'may never be disturbed or the land alienated'. The trustees were charged to 'dispose of the yearly rents and profits on every Christmas Day amongst sixteen poor persons in the almshouses founded by John and Ralph Skynner.'

Upon the enclosure of the parish of Ippollitts, half-an-acre of this land was taken by the Commissioners in consideration of the land being freed from tithes and towards defraying the expenses of the Act. The remaining land was intermixed with land belonging to Joseph Margetts Pierson. In 1895 the land was let at £3 per annum to Robert Harkness. It was subsequently sold and the proceeds invested in the name of the official trustee to produce an increased income.

In 1850 Laurence Wilshere, writing to 'Notes and Queries', stated that 'the gravestone was, till quite lately, a lion, in the neighbourhood, but a sacrilegious farmer, annoyed at the injury done to his hedges by the visitors to the tomb has either removed the stone or sunk it below the level of the ground'.

Cussens (History of Hertfordshire) says: A plain stone, bearing this inscription marked the place of Tristram's interment.

> M. S.
> R. T.
> AB ANNO MDCCXXXIV
> Requiescat in pace
>
> (Memoria Sacra)
> Sacred to the Memory
> Richard Tristram
> From the year 1734
> May he rest in Peace

This stone having fallen into decay a new memorial was erected in 1856 at the expense of Charles Wilshere.

For people wishing to learn more about the family of Tristram a visit to the Hertfordshire Record Office to see the pedigree is recommended.

Below: Tristram's grave today, the Oakfield estate is in the background.

WHITEHILL ROAD

Whitehill Road probably gets its name from being a hill and being chalky, hence white. It appears as a road, on an early nineteenth-century map of Hitchin and though it is not named as Whitehill Road, Whitehill Piece, a small portion of land in the vicinity is noted on the map.

The building of several large houses took place in the late nineteenth and early twentieth centuries, though on a 1912 postcard one can hardly see the houses for the trees! Whitehill Close is named after a grand house which stood here. The stables-cum-garages of several of the houses have since been converted to make them habitable, notably Orchard Lodge. Its driveway was formerly a cartway.

There are some turn-of-the-century workers' dwellings in the road. It is intriguing to consider that numbers 47 to 53, built in 1902 and called Coronation Place, have on them the inscription 'Whites Hill' and the builder's initials CWW. A search of contemporary directories of Hitchin has not revealed who this builder was, whether his claim was humorous and whimsical, well founded or simply a stonemason's error.

Whitehill Road - 1940's & 1950's

Memories of the Last Two Chimney Sweeps in Hitchin! (Brian Worbey and his cousin, Alec Worbey)

'The traffic calming scheme is probably one of the final chapters in Hitchin's most changed road. Until the 1950's children could play in the road and it was noted for there being only nine houses.

From the Stevenage Road, going towards Hitchin, there were no houses on the left hand side until No. 83, where Alec C Worbey still lives. The first house on the right was known as Webb's (1904 on the wall). David Monk, an itinerant pipe-layer, lived in a gypsy caravan in the field behind. The next house was half way up the hill, 'The Red House' was built for the Smyth family (farmers and solicitors). Further up, near the brow, down a long drive was Lambert's Lodge next to which was Cordell's House, where the Ransom family lived.

Gone now are Blundell's house and Odell's, who lived at the old White Hill Farm, though they didn't farm there anymore. Car spraying and general repairs were carried out there. This area is now 'The Beeches'. Opposite No. 83, still on the right-hand side, was Roberts, a solid square house. Mr Roberts was a real distinguished gentleman of the area.

Opposite the top of St John's Road is No. 38, known as Joyner's house, where the Worbey family lived and carried on a market gardening business on the area beside it known as 'The Gardens', there were others there too. Finally there was Lucas's house, on the opposite side of the road, with its distinctive 'dragon' on the roof – we never dared to go and get our ball back if it went over the high wall when we were playing.

With the coming of Stevenage New Town, Whitehill Road started to change, for workers found it was a shorter route from Walsworth, Ickleford etcetera, and it was also the start of development of the area.

Building began on the Oakfield Estate in the 1950s while the 1960s saw the development of Southill Close, the Wimpey Estate and Maytrees. Passingham Avenue was built on the site of a gravel pit, which used to supply the brickworks in St John's Road, at the end of the nineteenth century. When the pit fell into disuse my father built two large, 30 yds x 13 yds, (27.42 metres x 11.88 metres) wooden rhubarb-forcing sheds in the bottom, which were eventually filled in during the early 1950's. The site of the pit is now directly under the green play area between Passingham Avenue and Lovell Close.

The 1970s saw the completion of The Beeches (White Hill Farm and Blundell's) and building was recently completed in 1993 around Joyners' house, now called Acre Piece. We remember Benny's - a field off Broadmead; Spratt's Dell - now Southill Close; The Gardens, this was virtually all the Wimpey estate. We grew crops of outdoor rhubarb, cauliflowers, lettuce, early potatoes, with orchards of Cox's Orange Pippins and the two best strawberry beds in North Herts! A recognised local hobby was scrumping!

Opposite Joyners, next to No. 83, were two little allotments, Welch's and Cook's; Spicer's Field is now Whitehill School...all the Whitehill names gone forever. How many people know that 83 Whitehill Road was the Pay Office for the Gravel Pits in the area?'

Hitchin's last two chimney sweeps lived in Whitehill Road, Brian Worbey was a sweep in the 1950's with his cousin Len Springett, and another cousin Alec Worbey was Hitchin sweep from 1959 - 1991.'

Derek Larkins recalls that, in the early 1950s... 'Hitchin had a huge timber yard, it used to cut up large trees for coffin boards for the local undertakers amongst other products. It was owned and operated by Massey Brothers and was situated opposite The New Found Out public house in an area now occupied by office blocks called S D R C.

I used to drive a timber lorry and trailer that could be loaded over sixty feet long. To get into Massey's from the Bedford or Luton Roads I had to travel down Tilehouse Street, the main road in those days, into Bridge Street, up Hitchin Hill, and down to the timber yard. Heaven help me if I met one of those Birch Bros. coaches in Bridge Street! Opposite Massey's timber yard in Stevenage Road was a small shop where I used to buy drinks and eats. It is now number 161 Stevenage Road'.

Above left: The intriguing datestone!
Above right: Bob Worbey on his tractor in June 1935. He is cutting up all 40,000 of his strawberry plants ruined by a late frost.
Right: Photographed in 1940, a pill box partially obscures Joyner's House, built in the 1920s.

WHITE HILL HITCHIN.

Dear Mr L
    Received your card. Will you start about 5.30 on Sunday, weather permitting. Rather a nice view on this card, have you ever been that way. It leads to Highbury. Best Regards to you both.
        N.S.

Top: The distinctive outline of Whitehill road as it appeared in 1912 (note the message on the reverse).
Above: The march of progress! The same view in 1995.

HITCHIN'S BURIAL GROUNDS

The Cemetery

Although not strictly speaking a place of divine worship, the Cemetery claims our notice under the present chapter from the solemn and sacred character of the purpose to which it is set apart, – the burial of the dead. The Cemetery is pleasantly situated on Highbury, on the east side of the town. It was opened on the 3rd May 1857, and the church portion consecrated by the Lord Bishop of Rochester. The entrance to the Cemetery is by Hitchin Hill, Highbury Road and Park Street through the Sand Dells. The chapels are nearly in the centre of the ground. The Cemetery will, doubtless, be a favourite resort of those who love the tranquil retreat that forms the abode of the dead. Notwithstanding the melancholy interest that attaches to the spot – it may be visited with pleasure. Its walks are neatly kept; the beauty of the situation, and the extent of view around, rendering it an additional adornment to the town and neighbourhood. J G Hawkins, Esq., is the Clerk and Registrar to the Burial Board, and T Fells is the Lodge Keeper and Sexton.

1875 Hitchin Household Almanack & Directory

Although there is evidence of Romano-British and earlier occupation in the area of Hitchin, it would appear that the foundation of the town dates from the period of the Anglo-Saxon occupation. Hitchin's first burial ground would probably have been that of the Benedictine monastery dedicated to St Andrew which was founded on the site of the present parish church by the nobles of King Offa of Mercia in the year 792. Its graveyard was said to extend from the river to the Icknield Way. This would not have been the present Icknield Way but more likely the Roman road from Verulamium to Sandy which, it is believed, ran roughly along the line of Sun Street and Bancroft. Occasional finds of burials under buildings on the other side of Bancroft, however, suggest that the course of the road may have been slightly further west. Interments therefore took place in this ground for over a thousand years and, although it is now a closed churchyard, burials of cremated ashes still occasionally occur. What is now known as the Garden of Rest was added to the churchyard in about 1815 and was used briefly for burials until the opening of the cemetery forty two years later.

Over the centuries, of course, other burial grounds have been established in Hitchin. One such is that of the Society of Friends at the junction of Paynes Park and the Bedford Road. Initially the Quakers did not mark their graves with headstones but the practice grew up later of using small, simple stones such as can be seen in Hitchin. The building of the present Meeting House necessitated the removal of some of the stones, and they can now be seen where they were repositioned around the walls. The Tilehouse Street Baptist Church also had an extensive graveyard with some delightful memorials. Again, some of the burials were disinterred when Robert Tebbutt Court was built upon part of the land and some interesting lead coffin-plates were discovered which are now in Hitchin Museum. Particularly worthy of notice is the stone set into the west wall of the church:

'AGNES BEAUMONT OF EDWORTH BEDFORDSHIRE (afterwards MRS STORY) Became a member of the Church at Bedford Under the pastoral care of the Revd. JOHN BUNYAN Octr. 31st 1672 Died at HIGHGATE Novr. 23rd 1720 Aged 68 Years. And being brought to HITCHIN by her own desire. was interred in the adjoining Grounds. This stone was erected by Subscription in 1812. in respectful Remembrance of a person so justly celebrated for her eminent piety and remarkable Sufferings'.

Top and left: Funeral of the late Sarah Ivory at St. Mary's and later at the Cemetery in June 1935. The undertaker is Frank West.
Above: Memorial Card for Mary Ann Denniss who died 25th January 1901, aged 35 years.
Below left: Detail from an advertisement for George Kirby, Undertaker, 1926 Almanack and Directory.

The grounds of other places of worship, such as the churches of the Holy Saviour, St Faith, St Mark, the Walsworth Road Baptist and the Grace Baptist, have never been used for burial purposes. The former Wesleyan Chapel in Brand Street, however, did appear to have one or two graves in front of it, and a modern day myth seems to have arisen that Sainsbury's store on the site is experiencing problems with its lift because it is sinking into the graveyard. The church was, however, at the other end of the property from the lift shaft and, if it is indeed subsiding, it is more likely to be into the cellar of the former Chalkley's Garage! Another church which had its own burial ground was the Congregational Chapel in Queen Street. Some of its graves were disturbed by excavation for construction of the retaining wall at the rear of Cannon House. Workmen stored the displaced bones in a tea chest then left them at the church door for blessing and reburial. The land was later cleared when an office block was built upon the site. Also in Queen Street are said to be the plague pits, or mass graves of the victims of the plague, whose numbers once led to the street becoming known as Dead Street.

In 1852 Parliament enacted a Burial Act for London, followed the next year by another covering the rest of the country. These enabled local authorities to establish and maintain burial grounds, and it was under the 1853 Act that Hitchin Cemetery was set up in 1857. It was opened on the 3rd May of that year by the Lord Bishop of Rochester and originally offered the facilities of both Anglican and non-conformist chapels in the central building. One is now used as a workshop for the grounds maintenance staff. Initially the area available for burials was smaller than it is now, the remainder of the surrounding land being used for allotments which have, over the years, been incorporated into the cemetery.

A visitor walking around will see many names familiar to those with a knowledge of Hitchin and its history. Beside the lodge house, for example, is the corner set aside for the Delmé-Radcliffe family of the Priory, although Sir Ralph, the last of the line, is not here. Not far away is the memorial to William Maylin, the Hitchin centenarian, after whom Maylin Close in Walsworth is named. There is John Smith, 'For 47 years the faithful servant of John Hawkins Esq', who is mentioned by Reginald Hine in his book of Hitchin Worthies. Hawkins, who was a widower, would be invited out to dine five evenings a week and Smith would drive him out in the dog-cart; but when the time came to return home, Smith having been entertained in the servants' hall as adequately as his master in the dining room, Hawkins would say 'Give me the reins Smith, I know how drunk I am; I don't know how drunk you are'!

Of those lying close by we can learn something of their trades and occupations. While some headstones give very little information with which to flesh out the bones of those below, we learn from the memorials to both Thomas Taylor and James Baker that they were '... of this town, plumber...'. James Mills was '...of this town, veterinary surgeon...' and William Morgan had been, we are told, '....49 years sexton of this parish...'. Annie Foster was '... the beloved wife of John Foster, (coachsmith)', while any schoolteacher would be understandably envious of the eulogium composed by friends and neighbours of William Dawson.

' A native of Pirton in this county. The loving and revered teacher of three generations in the town and neighbourhood of Hitchin. A man of unspotted life whose high attainments were adorned by gentleness and modesty. A bright example of the domestic virtues. A sure friend and delightful companion. Died Feb 27th 1889 Aged 83'.

Some memorials give a more precise location than merely 'of this town'. There is 'Anne the beloved wife of John James of Orton Head', and 'Hannah the much loved wife of Willm. Arnold Chipperfield who died at Hitchin Hill', while one stone gives the full address: 'Mary Ann the beloved wife of William James Denniss of 51 Walsworth Road Hitchin Herts'. In similar vein is the memorial to young Margaret Todd and her family, but this is of interest in that it shows how the sons of

Hitchin were, in the nineteenth century, journeying the world to be of service in the British Empire and beyond:

'In loving remembrance of Margaret Callander Todd who died at Alma Villa Old Park Road Hitchin 28th March 1876. Aged 16 months. Also Thomas eldest son of William and Jeanie Todd who was killed by a fall from his horse at Grahamstown South Africa 21 Nov. 1891 In the 25th year of his age. Interred in the Scotch Cemetery Grahamstown. Also Jeanie the dearly beloved wife of William Todd who died 6th July 1906 aged 67. Also Andrew McMillan Todd. Second son of the above who died at Orange City Florida. USA on 9th December 1904 aged 36'.

We also find 'Louisa Stevens. Widow of the late James Stevens Esq. of the Bombay Civil Service'.

Travel was not only one way though: people moved into the town. The Todd family had probably originated in Scotland, and we find 'James Shilcock born at Donnington Lincolnshire...', 'William Masters. Late of Wood Green..' and even 'Frederick N Burt

formerly of Sydney N S W'. Among a line of war graves near to the Cemetery Road gate are two of a slightly different design from the remainder. They are the memorials to two young German airmen, Euerl Wolfgang and Anthony Georg, who died aged nineteen and twenty-seven respectively and now lie at rest with their former enemies.

Before the days of the female emancipation movement women were generally described, as we have seen, by reference to their husbands. In fact, their headstones often give more information about the man than his late wife, especially if he had been engaged in an occupation in the public eye. There is for example 'Ann the beloved wife of George Young. Late Police Inspector of this town....' and, on the St John's Road side of the cemetery, 'Elisabeth Therese. Wife of Jabez King MA Oxon. Headmaster Grammar School Hitchin'. Of all the epitaphs in this style, one to the south west of the lodge house which catches the eye is that to Anna, the daughter-in-law of the Reverend W Griffith of Hitchin:

'Anna (geb: Weidemann, aus Berlin) The faithful and dearly beloved wife of the Revd. Arthur Griffith Minister of Bishopsgate Chapel, London who died in Edinburgh March 1879. After giving birth to her fifth child. Aged 33. She hath done what she could'.

'Grieving Woman'. Monument to George Clark Payne and family, Hitchin Cemetery.

Appendix I

Building Hitchin

The market town of Hitchin lies within good and varied farming country, close to the ancient Icknield Way, on the River Hiz and with the firm foundation of the Chalk, all of which factors contributed to its success and development. However, there is much more variation to the surface geology than might at first be apparent, and it is this variety which enabled Hitchin to expand during the nineteenth century, largely using its own locally produced resources. The following extract of a 'Panoramic Survey' enlarges on this point and explains the presence of all the basic materials for building.

Extract from Handbook to Hitchin and the Neighbourhood 1891 Panoramic Survey

'The range of Chalk hills which outskirt the north of Hertfordshire are extremely interesting to the lovers of the picturesque and the student of nature. From the base of these hills numerous brooks and rills gently issue forth to fertilise the vales through which they flow, and by their united streams form the rivers Lea, Ivel and Cam. The deep bed of Gault Clay, which underlies the peaty soil of the fens and the sands of Bedfordshire, stretches up the valley of the Hiz, in which the town of Hitchin is built.

Children at work in the brickyard. Woodcut, late 18th century.

The line of demarcation which the Chalk makes is tolerably distinct. Verulam Road, Windmill Hill and Highbury to Ippollitts Brook on the east; Charlton to Orton Head on the west; the intermediate space being principally sand, gravel and clay.'

We extract the following interesting article from the Journal of the Hitchin Natural History Club (1891), by kind permission of Mr W Hill:-

OUR FORGOTTEN LAKE
A page from the Unwritten History of Hitchin.

In the south-east corner of the parish of Hitchin, in that part known as the Folly, are several brick-yards. These are situated on the southerly slope of an irregular ridge or spur running about north-east and south-west, which forms the eastern boundary of the valley in which Hitchin stands, and also the water-shed between the river Hiz and the rivulet known as Ippolyts Brook. This brook, joining forces with the Pur at Purwell Mill, passes round the extremity of the spur and becomes confluent with the Hiz at Grove Mill. From the higher portions of the spur, that is across the park, along the cemetery ridge towards Highbury and the station, the ground sinks rapidly towards the valley of the Hiz, but towards Ippolyts Brook the slope is more gradual, and the brick-yards are placed in a valley-like depression which runs at right angles to the direction of the ridge. The brickearth, which is, of course, the *raison d'etre* of the brick yards, is of a red brown colour, without perceptible stratification in the clay itself, but there occur layers in which small angular flints are very abundant, and these show plainly where, after the digging, the sides of the pits are left to the action of the weather. Besides these small flints, which are also sparsely scattered through the clay, there are comparatively few large stones in the brickearth. The brick-works commence just below Hitchin Cemetery, about two-thirds of the distance from the brook to the summit of the ridge. Descending the ridge by the footpath (Taylor's Hill) which leads to the Folly, the first excavations will be seen on the right and left (Messrs. Ransom's pits) immediately after crossing Brick-kiln Lane. It will be noticed that the clay has been dug here to a depth of twenty-five feet. Proceeding down the path towards the Folly, pits from which clay has been dug occur on either side for some distance, but they terminate in the small allotment gardens in the rear of the cottages at the Folly. Crossing the Stevenage Road, clay has again been dug at Mr Jeeves' brick-works. Here however it is only three to six feet thick, and looking from this point, it will be noted that the brick-earth thickens along the sides of the valley, and towards the summit of the ridge in proportion to the gradual rise of the ground. Throughout this area the depth to which the clay is dug is governed by a bed of curious character. This is a calcareous loam of a pale yellow ochreous colour, sometimes almost white at the top. Its thickness at Mr Jeeves' brick yard, where it can be seen to be underlain by some very coarse gravel, is about three feet, but in another part of the same yard, more to the west, the yellow loam passes down into a blackish earth unquestionably the same deposit, from its fossil contents. This was dug to twelve or fourteen feet without getting to the bottom. A well which was dug some years ago in Mr A Ransom's pit penetrated similar material without going through it.

What is this bed of calcareous loam? The first thing that will strike anyone who examines it is the number of shells it contains. The most common is a little bivalve, something like a cockle, and the small whorled shell of a snail. A conchologist would immediately recognise both as common in the rivers and ditches of the neighbourhood. A short search will disclose several more species, and an inspection of certain white lines will show that they are nothing less than beds of freshwater mussels so thickly placed as to form a regular layer. These freshwater forms can still be

Invoice dated 1891 for goods supplied to Whiteways Bottom Beer House

found alive and their dead shells in the mud at the bottom of rivers and ponds of our neighbourhood.

By the same token, a plant known as Ehara is said to have grown in the area because seeds have been found. Now only found round Scottish lochs, the conclusion must be that the climate was cooler in Hitchin once than it is now.

What then must we say of a deposit which contains shells, plants and other organic remains almost identical with those which we ourselves find in the mud of our rivers and ponds? There can only be one answer to this question which is this - the yellow loam at the Folly must be of fresh water origin. . . . . . .

Thus it would seem that at the brick-works at the Folly we have evidence that there existed here a body of quiet water, and that this must have remained in its place for a long period - a period sufficient for an accumulation of fresh water mud of at least twelve feet thick to have formed.

The impression of most people who have visited the brick yards is that the deposit was formed at the bottom of still water - in fact, a lake, and so to our collectors the loam is known as 'The Lake Bed'.

Such a lake would have been visited by elephants, rhinoceros, hippopotamus, bear and stag, and the remains of all these have been found.

The evidence as to the extent of the lake is incomplete. It seems most probable that its limit to the westward must have been the Highbury or Cemetery Ridge. The ridge or spur is nothing but a huge heap of water worn gravel and sand banked against a chalk knoll, which joins its north-eastern extremity and which can be seen at the station and at Whitehill.

The opening of the ground for laying sewers along the streets of Hitchin afforded a favourable opportunity for ascertaining the nature of the soil, which was as follows:-

Park Street Queen Street	}	*Sand*
Bridge Street Sun Street Bucklersbury Market Place Biggin Lane Back Street	}	*Sand with basins of chalk nodules*
High Street Bancroft Portmill Lane Church Yard	}	*Gravel*
Tilehouse Str.	>	*Sand*
West Lane and thence to Bearton	}	*Clay intermixed with stones*
Whinbush Road	>	*Gravel*
Starlings Bridge	>	*Gault with chalk nodules*
Radcliffe Road	>	*Chalk*

Some interesting discoveries of what Hitchin was like in the olden times were made during the excavations: in Bridge Street and Portmill Lane the stream was crossed by a ford, or washway, with only a foot bridge for passengers; near the Horse Pond and in Market Place, at the east corner, were thick layers of the horns of oxen, evidently placed there to form a foundation for the road in the same manner that faggots are used in the roads through woods, horns at that time being considered of but little value; a wall of

considerable height, entirely made of them, was in existence not many years ago against an excavation in the sand near the entrance to the town in Park Street. The remains of a Pilgrim's staff with spike and ferrule were found near the entrance to the Churchyard. In High Street, at the bottom of Brand Street (formerly a narrow entrance to the town, called Pound Lane), the bones of a horse which had been buried with its harness on, were found a little below the surface, probably owing to the bad state of the road it had met with an accident and been suffered to remain with only a slight covering of earth.

At the lower end of Bancroft the rivulet which flowed from Cap's Well down Silver Street (probably so called from the silvery appearance of the water caused by its reflecting the sun's rays at noon) joined the Hiz at Starlings Bridge, then only a foot bridge'. *Published by Paternoster & Hales, Hitchin, 1899.*

The Building Industry and Building Materials

The word 'brick' did not come into general use until the reign of Elizabeth I. 'Thacktills' (roofing tiles) 'Waltel' (wall tiles) 'Tequla' (bricks) and 'Tequlater' (bricklayer) were the terms used by the ancient craft.

Sands, gravels, clays for brickmaking (brickearths) and chalk for lime were all present in Hitchin and thus it is no surprise that local firms were not only builders but also extracted raw materials and were brickmakers as well as being joiners, carpenters and undertakers. Plumbers, glaziers and painters were often grouped together because their trades were routed in the manufacturing and repairing of leaded windows. Prior to the nineteenth century there was no building 'industry' as we know it today. Those engaged in building were tradesmen who, having served their apprenticeships, took pride in their crafts. They usually knew all the details of the business, especially if they were following in the family tradition.

An owner would make separate contracts with the different tradesmen needed in construction of a building. This began to change with the advent of Thomas Cubitt of Norwich, a carpenter, who found the system inconvenient. He founded the London Institution and employed all trades, consolidating them into one establishment. Gradually, as tasks overlapped, the men became 'master builders' instead of master carpenters, master bricklayers and so on. As the population of the town was ever on the increase more and more houses were built, so more co-ordinated methods of organising building were necessary and inevitable.

The building industry was one of the biggest industries in Hitchin throughout the nineteenth century. It employed 12% of the male population by the year 1901. Hitchin had plenty of raw materials right on the doorstep including lime from the chalk of the Chilterns, building sand from glacial gravels, bricks from local brickearths and timber, mainly oak and hornbeam, from the area of Redcoats Green. Trees were selected by the builder and merchant together, felled and taken to Hitchin by cart, where the sawyers cut them into sections. Although most builders had their own sawpit, not many employed their own sawmen, who would move from one yard to another just as sheep shearers move from farm to farm.

Most materials were conveyed by horse and cart. Items not available locally such as glass, lead and Welsh slate were imported. When the tipping cart was invented, work was completed more quickly because loads did not have to be shovelled out of the carts by hand. By and large building work was carried on in much the same way until some revolutionary discovery or invention changed things, for example, the industry was greatly affected by the coming of the railway in 1850, the electric telegraph in 1870 and the internal combustion engine thereafter.

Hitchin's sandpits were situated at the bottom of Hitchin Hill, (where Standhill Road now starts), the dell on Walsworth Road, (now the site of the open air theatre) and along Pirton Road. Lime came mostly from the Benslow area and lime burning provided a livelihood for some families up to the coming of the railway, when it declined until Alfred

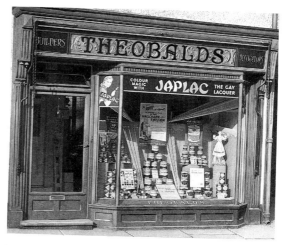

Shop fronting the firm's building premises in 28 Bancroft (1950s).

Ransom opened a limeworks in 1870 in Benslow cutting. Another lime works to the north of the station existed in Cadwell Lane and supplied many builders from the surrounding areas.

Alfred Ransom was also a brickmaker. His ancestors opened the brickfields in Sunnyside, (Bethel Lane, now St John's Road) which led to development of that part of the town. Most bricks were hand-made right up to the end of the nineteenth century.

Another firm which did its own lime burning and brick making was that of Jeeves. Ransom and Jeeves together were responsible, in large part, for the expansion of Hitchin as a town. Once Portland cement from Northfleet in Kent had been patented, it was some time before it was in great demand, but Alfred Ransom was just one agent through whom it was sold locally.

Tilehouse Street probably got its name from the tile making kiln that once stood near the top of the hill. Most tiles in Hitchin were locally made, often by brickmakers. Any iron fittings needed in the building of houses were readily supplied by local blacksmiths. Local materials were only slowly displaced after the coming of the railways opened up new sources of supply.

Many Hitchin houses also illustrate the trend for Victorian architects to imitate features of earlier Gothic churches and cathedrals. In contrast with the very plain exteriors of the previous age, much superfluous ornamentation was now added to the new houses. Stucco was becoming unfashionable by the 1850's and various odd forms and mouldings were added to otherwise plain brick exterior walls to relieve the monotony.

In Hitchin, many of the better houses built in the latter half of the nineteenth century boast such details. Terracotta was increasingly used as the century advanced and both floor and roof tiles were widely made from this material. The front elevation of Hitchin Post Office was faced with terracotta when it was built in 1904. Many of the larger Hitchin houses of this period had chequered pattern tiled floors.

The formal, balanced elevation that distinguished houses of the classic age was now completely abandoned, and many of the larger houses were built almost without regard to anything save the whim of the owner.

The Builders

One thing is certain – the building industry never stood still. It had to adapt to change whenever new laws were made; for instance various Public Health Acts meant that higher standards of hygiene had to be met and the Torrens Act of 1868 laid the foundation of much subsequent legislation on housing being fit for human habitation. The Hitchin Local Board, later the Urban District Council, owed its powers to make by-laws to the Public Health Act of 1875 and the granting of planning permission after the submission of plans by builders is rooted here.

Mr Anthony Foster points out that Mr George Jeeves once fell foul of these by-laws when he tried to build some cottages in Russell's Slip without the required permission. The Local Board would not allow him to proceed until plans were approved. When the plans were deposited the Board visited the site and insisted on modifications to room heights and the drainage arrangements.

Jeeves – Builders

The influence of the Ransom family is fairly well documented already as the firm of Ransom is still in business; but the legacy of the Jeeves family, so important in the construction of Victorian Hitchin, is less well-known. It is thought that Messrs Jeeves were the largest builders in the nineteenth century and the first firm to be called builders but sadly they are now all gone. They developed the Highbury area and much of Walsworth Road. The Baptist Church, on the corner of these two roads, was built by George Jeeves in the neo-Gothic style between 1875 and 1876 with seating for five hundred people. It had a gallery at the rear and a splendid window to the north-west. At the time of writing the firm of Archer is about to commence cleaning and restoration of the stonework. It replaced an earlier mission hall built by Richard Johnson, the railway engineer, out of concern for the spiritual needs of the railway workers. Jeeves also completely rebuilt the girls' and infants' sections of the British Schools in 1857 - the building which now faces onto Queen Street.

The Jeeves family was large and included more than one builder. A notice preserved in the museum is said to have appeared in Messrs Jeeves yard in the 1860's and reads thus:

> 'Honesty is the best policy'-
> 'Do unto others as you would wish
> others to do to you'

These precepts were followed by seven strict rules for his workmen to observe. The fact that it refers to Messrs Jeeves is an indication that George's cousin Frederick was already working with him as his foreman, but later Frederick set up in business on his own account at 110 Walsworth Road, premises occupied afterwards by Willmott. Frederick undertook the building of the shaft at Ransom's distillery and built the bridge over the River Hiz when Hermitage Road was opened. He was an adherent of the strict Baptist cause, worshipping at Bethel Chapel where he did some preaching as a supply teacher. He was

*Manhole covers
proclaiming the
names of local
builders often
giving a clue
about the
construction of a
particular house.*

married twice and is buried with his second wife Winifred and daughter Lizzie at Hitchin Cemetery. He was in his 83rd year when he died in 1910 and Lizzie had reached 95 years of age when she died in 1959.

George Jeeves was born in 1822 and died in 1896. He had at least three brothers, Edward, William and Thomas. His father was William Jeeves who married one of Thomas Topham's daughters. George set up his building firm at 40 Queen Street and worked for some time with his cousin Frederick. His wife was called Martha. They produced a family of six daughters and three sons; Emily, Rose, Alice,

Annie Louise, Ada and Constance, Walter, William and George Edward. Emily died in 1860 at the age of twelve.

George Jeeves is known to have laid down strict rules for his workers regarding punctuality, absence, drinking and petty theft. There were probably no active local unions to question the fines he imposed if rules were breached. However, his obituary records that he believed in rewarding diligence as 'he gives two cottages at Charlton to George Walls and James Masters, two mechanics in the employ of his son Walter, in recognition of their good conduct and attention to business'.

William Jeeves, George's brother, set up as an undertaker, and that business included all three of his sons; Moses, Edward and W J Jeeves. A daughter, Clara, died in her thirties. William was born in 1823 and died in 1904 leaving his sons to carry on the firm of W Jeeves & Sons. Buried with William is his wife Ann, Clara and Moses, who died in 1925.

George Jeeves' son Walter took over from him at Queen Street. In 1899 he married Isabel Louise Barnes, only daughter of Samuel West Barnes of Ashford in Kent, at the Congregational Church in Westminster with the Reverend C T Bryer of Hitchin officiating. A dinner was held for ninety guests afterwards at the Sun Hotel. In the Chair was Lawson Thompson and other guests included James Shilcock and W J Fitch. It must have been a fairly lighthearted affair as songs were sung by Moses Jeeves and his employees. Walter and Isabel had at least two children. He lived a while on Wymondley Road but had retired to Dyxcroft, Rottingdean in Sussex by the time he died in 1922 – which also seems to be the date of the demise of the building firm.

Walter's two brothers, William, who was an architect and builder, and George Edward, who lived at Highbury, may have been involved in the trade. A list of planning applications shows that William was building in the following places:

Taylor's Lane 1887, two cottages; Park Road 1888, new stables; Market Place 1899, new building for Innes & Co. ; High Street 1899, alterations for Latchmore; Exchange Yard 1899, alterations for Carling; 9 Highbury Road, 10 Nettledell Road 1900, two villas; Market Place 1902, alterations to the Rose and Crown.

He also built several houses in Old Park Road, Lancaster Road and Blackhorse Lane, one house in Storehouse Lane in 1902, one in Nettledell Road (now Highbury) in 1901 and the Lawson Thompson house in The Avenue in 1901. Walter Jeeves was responsible for building a garage at The Hoo in 1913 and E E Jeeves was production architect for a house in The Avenue in 1928 and a shop in Queen Street in 1927. Other houses in The Avenue

were built by F Newton, J Knight, W French, F W Kinneir-Tarte and M & F O Foster.

There were members of the Jeeves family who were not builders. Henry and Alfred, sons of James Cawdell Jeeves (who was a builder), both went to work at Hawkins' in Portmill Lane. Henry, who lived at 15 Bedford Road, worked there for sixty years. Like his father before him, he was an attached member of Tilehouse Street Baptist Church. His brother, Alfred Jeeves, moved from Hawkins after 1870 to Messrs. Walters & Co., Solicitors of Lincoln's Inn, where he remained until his retirement in 1903. He resided at Finsbury Park but he is buried in Hitchin Cemetery with his wife Ann. Their daughter, Miriam Lewin Phillips, lies with them but their son, F A Jeeves, has proved elusive. Henry Jeeves had six children but only one daughter seems to have stayed in the area. She became Mrs Collier and lived in Old Park Road.

At the time of Henry's death, his eldest son was in business in New York. Who knows? He may have set up as a builder!

Of course, many other building firms were involved in the growth of Hitchin. More information about some of these firms can be found in the sections of this book which deal with the particular streets where their headquarters were located.

Francis Newton	Tilehouse Street
F Wells	Old Park Road
Pettengell & Co	Strathmore Avenue
(Pettengell & Clark)	
M & F O Foster	York Road
J Willmott & Sons	Walsworth Road

Manhole Covers

No single company of builders was dominant in the rapid expansion of Hitchin during Victorian and Edwardian times. The Hitchin Household Almanack of 1915 lists a large number of builders. Clearly they were all proud of their work and achievements and a common form of advertising was to cast manhole covers bearing the name of the company. These have been cast by the local ironfounders. As the photographs on page 167 show, many of these covers still exist.

Appendix II

SOME LOCAL IRONFOUNDERS

The Worshipful Company of Ironmongers, one of twelve great City guilds, was founded before 1348. Hardware, meaning ironmongery or small goods or wares of metal, is a term which was first used in about 1515. With the Industrial Revolution and its concentration of the metal industry well under way during the nineteenth century, it is hardly surprising that ironmongers provided the bulk of household goods in use, both indoor and outdoor, with a large range from which to choose.

Hitchin itself is not now regarded as a town founded on the iron making or engineering industries but it had its fair share of works and employers in those industries, many of whom concentrated on the increasing degree of mechanisation within agriculture.

Robert Isaac's Family and Foundry

Five generations of the Isaac family have worked their foundry at St Ippolyts on the outskirts of Hitchin since it was established in 1865. The founder, Robert Isaac (1830 - 1895) son of John Isaac (an iron founder) and Mary was living in Puckeridge (census 1841) and in Hertford (1851). Robert married Mary Olney in 1852 at St Ippolyts . He was victualler at The Greyhound (Cravens Directory 1853) and started his own foundry business in a barn at the rear. He then rented a dwelling, outbuildings and land at Brook End, from Elizabeth Thorpe of Hitchin and established the family business on its present site. His business card reads:-

---

Robert Isaac
Iron & Brass Founder
Hitchin
Castings of Iron & Brass made to order of
every description

One of the reasons for starting an iron foundry in a country area was to serve the

Extracts from the Hitchin Census 1881

Name	Age	Occupation	Born	Street
Bowler John	25	Blacksmith	Hitchin	Brand Street
Bowler William	20	Blacksmith	Hitchin	Brand Street
Cain Thomas	52	Blacksmith	Evershall	Crabs Close
Cooper Charles	26	Blacksmith	Leighton Buzzard	Gascoines Yard Back Street
Emery Edward	23	Blacksmith	Baldock	Portmill Lane
Gatward John	54	Ironmonger/Watchmaker	Hitchin	Cock Street
Gatward John Junior	28	Ironmonger	Hitchin	Quakers Alley
Girling Henry	20	Ironmonger's Assistant	St Ives	Quakers Alley
Hide Henry	17	Ironmonger's Lab.	Hitchin	Quakers Alley
Paternoster Charles	23	Ironmonger's Assistant	Hitchin	Market Place
Perkins Thomas	29	Ironmonger	Hillmorton Warwick	Market Place
Rackwood Robert	28	Blacksmith	Norfolk	Highbury
Roberts Richard	57	Iron Moulder	East Indies	Market Place
Roberts Thomas	17	Iron Founder	Hitchin	Old Park Road
Rogers George	16	Ironmonger's Assistant	Hitchin	Cock Street
Rogers Mary W	44	Ironmonger, *(employing two men)*	Kinsale Ireland	Cock Street
Sale John	58	Blacksmith	Biggleswade	Quakers Alley
Walton Jonathan	32	Moulder	Gloucestershire	Market Place
Worsley George	35	Ironfounder's Lab.	Hitchin	Back Street

local farming community. In the early days customers were drawn from a radius in which a horse and cart could deliver in a day.

Robert and Mary Isaac had a family of twelve (1861 census and onwards). Henry Isaac (1865-1958) was the sixth son and he began to enlarge the type of work to include engineering castings and this gradually became more important for the firm as the needs of agriculture decreased. On a horse plough there were at least twelve different parts made of cast iron but as tractors and their ploughs, made mostly of steel, took over, the need for cast iron parts lessened. Henry used to send his hand-written bills out once a year, around Christmas time. He would have an old wicker basket full of them ready for sending out. He would then go down to Hitchin market in February to collect, a very different way of doing business in his day! Henry Isaac, after whom the firm is named, was a great local character, independent, cussed and determined. He was still working in the foundry when he was eighty-four.

Today the link continues with the manufacture of components for agricultural machinery such as tractor weights, Cambridge rolls and Land packers; engineering and ornamental castings are also made. Fabricated steel work is supplied to the building trade and general repair work is carried out.

An example of Perkins' ironware once stood in E A Primes's Garage, Queen Street. It was probably used as a drinking trough.

From Small Beginnings: The Influence of Thomas Perkins

Thomas Perkins was of farming stock and hailed from Warwickshire. He was left fatherless when young and was apprenticed into the ironmongery trade. Arriving in Hitchin at the age of twenty-seven he set up his ironmongery and engineering business in Exchange Yard. In 1856 he married Frances Sharman of Wellingborough, whose father, John Wood Sharman, was also an ironmonger.

The enterprise thrived and expanded with the coming of the railway, this was the age of iron and steam and Thomas used it to benefit farmers with his agricultural machinery. By now he probably had his offices and showrooms by the Corn Exchange calling himself a 'Furnishing Ironmonger, Iron Merchant and Agricultural Implement Manufacturer'. His works in Bancroft produced stationary engines for agricultural use, stackers, hay and straw elevators, kitchen ranges and iron bedsteads.

In 1858 John Sharman became a Trustee of the Queen Street Ironworks in Peterborough. The manager, William Barford, took on the lease with his partner Thomas Amies. Barford dealt with the Ironworks and Amies managed the Ironmongery. A method of weighting road rollers with water ballast was patented by Barford in 1862.

Perkins, too, was busy inventing ploughs, reapers and mowers. Both men exhibited regularly at the Royal Agricultural Show and with John Sharman as the 'link man' they would have got to know each other. Thus in 1865 the firm became 'Amies, Barford & Co.' but Perkins remained in Hitchin. He had plenty of work maintaining his steam engines used in ploughing, in 1870 his newly-patented Double Farrow Plough competed in trials at Peterborough and in the same year he patented folding shafts for reapers and mowers.

The Amies and Barford partnership was dissolved in 1872 with no apparent animosity and a new partnership formed between Barford and Perkins. In the same year Perkins took into partnership Charles Paternoster and

Samuel Burlingham at the Hitchin end. This was when the business in Hitchin became 'Perkins & Company' with the works in Exchange Buildings becoming 'The Hitchin Ironworks'. The year 1872 was also important for marketing a new invention called 'Perkins New Patent Combines Stacker & Straw Elevator' which led the way towards the firm becomming a world leader in mechanical handling. As Thomas Perkins became less active the firm again altered its name to 'Perkins, Paternoster & Burlingham'.

The Peterborough company tried to produce their first steam roller in 1887 by linking a steam engine to water ballasted rollers but Aveling & Porter of Rochester were ahead of them. Nevertheless Barford and Perkins' brick-making equipment for the Fletton Brick Industry was much in demand as the rate of house building grew.

Thomas Perkins bought George Kershaw's house, Charnwood, in 1860 and it seems fitting that this house is now Hitchin Museum. His eldest son, John Edward Sharman Perkins,

A circular pig trough last made in the 1950s by Isaacs and still in use today.

graduated at King's College, London and joined Barford & Perkins at Peterborough in 1884 as a skilled engineer. The firm expanded producing steam engines, road rollers and brick-making machinery. When William Barford died in 1898 his son, James Goldly Barford, took on the succession but Thomas Perkins was still head of the firm and

Tapping the furnace at Henry Isaac's foundry at St Ippolyts, in the 1980s.

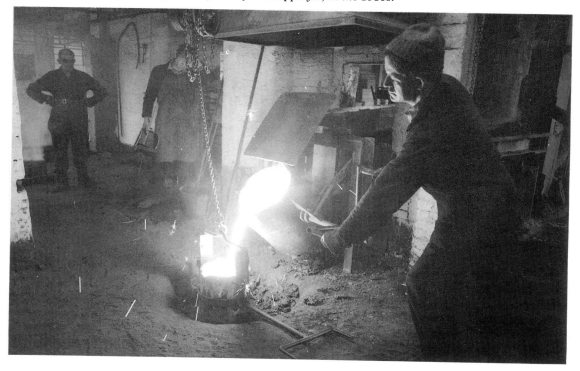

Gatward's premises in the High Street. On the extreme left was The Swan, sold to the firm in 1884.

Ironmongers - Gatward - Ironfounders

John Gatward & Sons was a firm of engineers established in 1835. The ironmongery store stood on the High Street side of the entrance to the Swan Inn yard and an iron foundry was run from the Swan yard behind what we now know as The Arcade. According to Anthony Foster, a great fire occurred on the night of 22 March 1853 '...at Gatward's furnishing and ironmongery warehouse in High Street in which the owner's wife was burned to death'. There were 130 pounds of gunpowder on the site at the time and the premises were destroyed.

When the Swan closed in 1884 it was bought and modified by John Gatward. By adding a glazed roof he was able to use the enclosed area as a furniture showroom. He sold 'good and cheap suites of furniture for sitting rooms and bedrooms, bedsteads and bedding, mail carts and perambulators, easy chairs etc'.

By 1899 Messrs John Gatward & Sons Ltd continued so until his death in 1908, when his son, J E S Perkins, and J G Barford became Joint Managing Directors.

The Peterborough company and its competitor, Aveling & Porter, became part of Amalgamated General Engineers after World War One. John Perkins and his son Frank began to produce diesel engines after 1932 and Barford joined up with Aveling to form a limited company. Perkins Engines Ltd. of Peterborough, Aveling Barford Ltd. of Grantham and Innes King, later Geo. W King Ltd are famous throughout the world for engines, road rollers and mechanical handling. They are all a tribute to Thomas Perkins, one of Hitchin's engineers.

Page from a trade catalogue used by Thomas Brooker and Sons in the 1930s.

Left: Handsome footscraper to be found in Bancroft, and drawn by Becky Hull.

were noted as manufacturers of agricultural implements selling corn and seed drills, and under Royal Patronage. The firm appears listed both as Ironfounders and Ironmongers in the Hitchin Almanack for 1926 but it closed very soon after. It was sold to make way for the shopping arcade which opened in 1927.

Other ironfounders also produced urban hardware in Hitchin. Details of their activities are described in the sections on the streets which held their main offices - G H Innes and Geo. W King, both in Walsworth Road.

Footscrapers

Much exterior hardware and ironmongery has been made in Hitchin. However one item which became common outside Victorian front doors, the footscraper, seems to have been rather specialist and was mainly manufactured elsewhere. We know of only one type of scraper made locally by John Gatward. Designs from two suppliers to Thomas Brooker & Sons are pictured here and several examples can still be found beside Hitchin front doors. They occur in some older streets, with definite correlation between more prestigious houses and more elaborate scrapers.

Thomas Brooker & Sons, who had branches in Leys Avenue, Letchworth, and Walsworth Road, Hitchin at the time, used the catalogues of Thomas Holcroft & Sons Ltd., Wolverhampton and A Kenrick & Sons Ltd., West Bromwich, during the 1930's from which they supplied local builders.

BIBLIOGRAPHY

Aberdein A. *Short History of Caldicott School 1984*
Curtis G. *A Chronicle of Small Beer: The Early Victorian Diaries of a Hertfordshire Brewer.* Phillimore
Cussans J. K. *History of Hertfordshire.*
Dargent L. *A Walk Around Hitchin.* G P R Printing
Delderfield E. R. *Brief Guide to Inn Signs.* The Raleigh Press
Edwards D. F. *Hitchin in Old Postcards.* European Library
Ekwall G. *Concise Oxford Dictionary of English Place Names 1987*
Eyles A. and Skone K. *The Cinemas of Hertfordshire.* Herts Publications & Premier Bioscope
Field R. *Hitchin: A Pictorial History.* Phillimore
Fleck A. *Hertfordshire 1839-1914.* Countryside Books
Fleck A. *A Century in Camera.* Quotes Ltd
Fleck A. *Hitchin in Camera.* Quotes Ltd.
Fleck A. *Hitchin in Old Photographs.* Alan Sutton
Fletcher V. *Chimney Pots and Stacks.* Contour Press 1994
Foster A. M. *Market Town.* E. & E. Plumridge Ltd
Foster A. M. *The Book of Hitchin.* Barracuda Books Ltd
Foster A. M. *A Brief History of Hitchin Markets & Fairs.* Hitchin Historical Society and NHDC Museum Service
Gadd P. *Hitchin Past and Present.* White Crescent Press
Gadd P. *Hitchin Public Houses* (MS only)
Gadd P. and Pigram R. *Hitchin Inns and Incidents*
Hedges A. A. C. *Bottles and Bottle Collecting.* Shire Publications Ltd
Hine R. L. *Hitchin Old and New*
Hine R. L. *Hitchin Worthies.* E. T. Moore
Hine R. L. *Relics of an Uncommon Attorney.* J. M. Dent & Sons Ltd
Hine R. L. *Confessions of an Uncommon Attorney.* J. M. Dent & Sons Ltd
Hine R. L. *The Story of Hitchin Town.* Wm. Carling & Co Ltd.

Hine R. L. *The Hitchin Countryside.* Wm. Carling & Co Ltd
Hine R. L. *Samual Lucas His Life and Art Work.* Walkers Galleries Ltd
Hitchin Historical Society. *Old Hitchin Life Series,* Codicote Press
Hitchin Historical Society, *Hitchin Journals Hitchin Directories 1915-1965 Hitchin Official Guides and Handbooks 1875-1994*
Johnson W. B. *Hertfordshire Inns Part 1.* Hertfordshire Countryside
Latchmore E. A. *People, Places and Past Times of Hitchin.* D. P. Media
Lewis R. R. *A Hertfordshire Pharmaceutical Museum.* Hertfordshire Countryside
Offer C. *King Offa in Hitchin.* 1992
Pigram R. *Strange Happenings in Hitchin and North Herts 1978*
Poole H. and Fleck A. *Old Hitchin.* Eric T. Moore.
Walmsley R. *Around 1919.* Authorgraphics 1979
Whitmore R. *Of Uncommon Interest.* Spurbooks Ltd

OTHER SOURCES

Hitchin Museum: *Census Returns, Builders' Planning Applications, Lawson Thomson Scrapbooks*
Newspapers: *The Comet, The Herts Express, The Hitchin Gazette*
Pamphlets & Brochures: *Tromans F. A.: The Hitchin Cricket Club: A short history Hitchin Pageant Souvenir Programme 1951, Hitchin Town Supporters Club Annual 1957/58, Thespians Victoria's Diamond Jubilee Programme 1897*
Trade Catalogues: *Broad & Co Ltd., London. 1910 (in Hitchin Museum), F. Newton circa 1908. Lent by T. Brooker & Sons Ltd: Thomas Holcroft & Sons Ltd (West Bromwich) 1930's, Nicholls & Clarke Ltd.*
Maps: *Old Ordnance Survey Map: Hitchin 1898, Introduction by Steve Fletcher. Godfrey Edition.*

Index

Page numbers in *italic* refer to illustrations